CW00843143

STAYING TOGETHER

Secrets of a Successful Relationship

STAYING TOGETHER

Secrets of a Successful Relationship

Belinda Hollyer

Piccadilly Press · London

Phototypeset by Goodfellow & Egan, Cambridge
Printed and Bound in Great Britain by
Hartnolls Limited, Bodmin, Cornwall.
for the publishers, Piccadilly Press Ltd,
5 Castle Road, London NW1 8PR

A catalogue record for this book is available from the British Library

ISBN 1-85340-205-2

Belinda Hollyer lives in North London. She worked in publishing for many years and is now a freelance editor and writer.

INTRODUCTORY NOTE

All of the names listed below are pseudonyms, given to those I interviewed whilst preparing this book. Some of the people I interviewed were well-known to me; others were strangers. I am grateful to them all for the time they gave and the thoughts they shared with me, and I should like to dedicate this book to their generosity and their patience.

To Anna and Martin; Barbara; Carol and Alan; Claire and Chris; Eileen and Michael; Erica and Tom; Gordon; Helen and Peter; Jan; Jean and Danny; John and Sally; Kate and Ross; Keith; Louise and George; Robin and Brian; Sarah; Sue and David; and Sylvia.

Contents

INTRODUCTION

When I began work on this book, I thought it was perfectly possible that I'd be able to pinpoint the secrets to having successful relationships. But I also thought the secrets were probably quite complicated ones – or, at least, a bit mysterious. After all, some people are much better at one-to-one relationships than others, but everybody tries quite hard to make their own relationships work. So why do some succeed, and others fail? Why do some people apparently handle the intimacies and demands of close relationships so much better than others?

I did a lot of reading, and I talked to a lot of people, and in the end, I realised that the secrets have been known to us all along. They are available to everyone. They are no more (or less) mysterious than the meaning we give to them. But many of us have great trouble in acknowledging their existence.

The couples I talked to are able to use their

differences in positive ways, and to generate intimacy and good humour between them. They treat each other well, with respect and affection, and they work hard to bring out feelings of affinity and trust in themselves and in their partners. The high levels of goodwill they share tend to insulate them against bad times, and help them to put their mistakes right – and then to put the mistakes behind them.

And the world responds more positively to couples who function at this level – just as it does to individuals who project positive feelings. The security, mutual enjoyment and generosity of spirit which such couples display creates its own goodwill. Their relationships seem to be charmed.

But such relationships are not enchanted; rather, they are the result of a combination of goodwill, self-knowledge, hard work and loving kindness. These qualities are available to us all.

You may think this all sounds easier in theory than it is in practice – and I agree. Committed relationships inside and outside marriage have not always been happy or successful experiences for me, and I'm still learning how to make my present one work – but I had a lot of ground to make up, and a lot of learning to do. And getting the details right while concentrating on the whole picture is a real skill. It certainly takes time and trouble, and probably at least some pain. I believe it's worth the effort.

THE MATING GAME

How do I love thee? Let me count the ways.
Elizabeth Barrett Browning

Chapter One

The Mating Game

A. Where It All Starts

1. ROMANTIC LOVE

"We discovered so many things together," Jean remembers with a smile, *"favourite travel writers, and cross-country skiing, and the best version of Handel's* Messiah, *and the easiest way to bake a whole salmon trout. We created our own little private world, and withdrew into it together. We both still had friends and jobs and so on, but* nothing *mattered in the same way as we did to each other – when we were together, everything felt more real."*

Jean is a successful management accountant in her early forties, and has lived with Danny for almost six years: before that, she'd had a series of relatively short-lived affairs. When they met, Jean fell in love with him almost immediately, and he with her.

About four months later, they decided to live together. Jean thought all her dearest wishes had come true.

But a year or so later, that first intensity began to fade. Jean recalls sitting at the breakfast table with Danny one morning, and suddenly feeling as though he had become a complete stranger to her. *"I looked at him across the jars of muesli and marmalade,"* she recounted, *"and an icy hand clutched at my heart. This hearty, self-absorbed man who chewed so loudly and smeared crumbs on the newspaper: was he really the man of my dreams; the man I had fallen so completely in love with such a little time ago?"*

The trouble with romantic love, as most of us discover at some stage of our lives, is that ordinary life seldom lives up to its breathtaking charms. Jean's case is not very different from many others of her age and background, and most of us will recognise the joys of romantic love – when the sun never seems to set, and when, as one woman put it, *"all I remember are golden days when we went for long walks and never once needed an umbrella or a raincoat."* But we also recognise that stage when the initial romantic attachment begins to loosen its powerful and passionate grasp on the heart; when reality begins to intrude; when a kind of psychic separation back into two individuals capable of separate desires and separate lives, begins to reassert itself.

Danny, Jean's lover, felt a similar 'withdrawal' from the first heady excitements. *"It was like a shift of perspective,"* he said. *"It wasn't that I stopped loving Jean, or stopped fancying her, or anything as definite as that. My feelings just seemed to lose the sharp focus they'd had to start with, and became a bit blurred. If we hadn't been compatible – if we hadn't had other things going for us, I mean – I'm not sure that we would necessarily have stayed together for very long after that time."*

2. BACK TO REALITY

The adjustment mostly seems to happen within the first few years of an attachment, although for Eileen and Michael, both professional writers now in their late forties, the separation took much longer.

"It wasn't really until I stood up from the nappy bucket, after about twelve years of an intensely involved

closeness to Michael, that I began to search for a separate role, and a different identity from the one I had in our relationship," Eileen explained. *"And it wasn't until a new research job took me away from home for several months, a few years after that, that I began to change and grow in an individual way again, as I had before I met Michael. Our marriage was never the same again – but it was the better for the change, not worse."*

3. THE INTENSITY OF INFATUATION

In our teens and twenties we tend to forge one-to-one relationships based on romantic attraction – and when that attraction fades, we tend to move on to the next infatuation. The knee-weakening, rapturous excitement of sexual desire is what sustains most of these infatuations, and that tidal wave of exhilaration is a powerful and absorbing experience.

Often, it's only later in life that we accept that there's a difference between being in love and loving, and that we begin to value potential partners for characteristics other than their overt sex appeal. It's no coincidence that *this* stage tends to coincide with a more settled search for a partner – or for more meaning in an existing or a new partnership – in our thirties and forties.

If we've picked well – or fortunately – then the choices we make with the heat of infatuated delight might be sustained through time. If we were initially swept away by desire and later discover that the continuing reality offers nothing more, however, we're more likely to put it down to experience, let go, and move on.

Of course, it's not only lust which determines early attachments – nor is it just our early choices which don't wear well. Relationships, we're constantly told, work best when the people in them are more alike than different, and so factors like similar backgrounds and personality traits, shared or interlocking interests, friends and values in common, even joint leisure activities, all play a part in helping them to succeed. But finding a truly compatible partner doesn't necessarily mean that we should search for a mirror-image of ourselves, nor that, if we do find similarity – or someone who fits our dearest fantasies – we'll achieve lasting happiness.

B. Aspects Of Love

1. TALL, DARK AND HANDSOME WILL DO FINE

Most people, it seems, begin with an initial basis of physical attraction, and move on from there. At a conscious level it may be no more specific a 'choice' than "I liked the way he looked" – although some psychologists believe that these first impressions also carry a heavy weight of hidden messages about similarity and difference: *"We marry,"* one said, *"to enhance our inner, largely secret selves."* We might, for example, appear to pick someone on the grounds of physical attraction, or "because he was around" – and only later discover an uncanny similarity of childhood experiences between us, which points to a much deeper reason for attachment.

Or, a related theory suggests, we might 'recognise' on some unconscious level that this potential partner fulfils our need to be looked after – maybe because their looks remind us of someone caring in our past.

2. THE SAME AGAIN, PLEASE

We all know people who seem constantly to replace, say, the pretty blonde weight-lifter in their life with another, seemingly identical one. This use of a pre-determined template of acceptable characteristics has more in common with an ideal fantasy-figure than with a sober and fulfilling reality, but it's a powerful influence in many people's lives.

"I could never like a man with brown eyes," Carol, a journalist in her early forties, told me. And she continued to describe a remarkably precise physical 'type' whom she believed she could find attractive, as well as an equally detailed one she found a turn-off. Of course, such fantasising can be delightful and entertaining – but it can also hinder, rather than help, the task of finding someone who's truly compatible with you. If you have such definite views as Carol, you might find it useful to spend time trying to remember when and where the ideal began to exercise its power. Did it begin with a pop-star from your teens? A crush at school? And does that ideal serve you well now you're an adult?

3. A DEAD-END FANTASY?

Sometimes, the fantasies associated with a certain set of characteristics drive us into dead-end relationships, and it's often only in retrospect that we can understand what went 'wrong'. Jean reflected how this had worked for her.

"It's interesting for me to look back on past relationships, and to see that when I was in my teens and twenties, I used only to be attracted to men who were, in conventional terms, very handsome. It wasn't a conscious thing at all, but it was absolutely there. I think that I must have seen them as a status prize: people would value me if they valued who I was with. Only when I gained confidence and authority in my own life, did my choice of men begin to reflect more interesting characteristics than their status as hunks!"

From her student days, Louise – now in her middle forties and married for the second time – remembers a rejected lover complaining that she only let men into her bed who'd passed a test on the Communist Manifesto! *"It was even more true than he realised: I was genuinely only attracted to men if I approved of their political opinions. Now, I find that idea uncomfortably close to a sort of quest in a fairy tale, and I don't need a mirror image of myself any more; in fact, I'm more interested in differences. But then, I found it disturbing and threatening to be confronted with the intellectual or emotional challenge involved in political variety. I badly needed the reassurance of agreement – and, if I'm really honest, I needed the authority of male approval for my beliefs, too."*

C. SO WHAT MAKES IT WORK, THEN?

1. COMPROMISE

One centrally important element of any successful relationship will certainly be compromise. Learning about give and take can be more difficult than you expect, especially if you have spent a large part of your adult life living alone and pleasing yourself, as Martin, a trade development expert, found when he married for the first time at forty-five.

"I had a rather idealised concept of marriage," he admitted, *"and the nuts and bolts of it were rather different! There were times when I was rather alarmed at how petty some of the difficulties seemed to be; now, I*

see that little things can assume an importance beyond what's reasonable, if the big things aren't tackled squarely. I try to keep my eye on what's really important – the security of the marriage; the future of my children – and that helps to ease me through the tangle of old habits and assumptions."

2. HARMONIOUS SPACE-SHARING

Successful relationships depend more on finding a way to exist in harmony with someone else's space than on meeting an idealised someone you can't live without: indeed, finding someone you can successfully live *with* may be more of a problem, especially if you are locked into a search for a pre-determined type.

Real compatibility needs to be built on more than physical attractions; more than the fulfilment of an ideal type – whether you seek someone to make up for characteristics you think you lack, or someone who affirms your idea of yourself as lovable, or maybe someone who nurtures you (or who submits happily to your nurturing needs).

There's nothing inherently *wrong* with those

ideas; it's just that they aren't guaranteed to be lasting or enduring ones. But there *are* no guarantees, you might object – and of course that's true. However, a relationship built on a shaky or a transient foundation needs a great deal of work if it's to get beyond its original function of playing out the fantasies of one or both the partners. Being looked after, for example, is lovely – but if it's carried to an extreme, or if it's carried on after your need has outgrown the situation, being looked after can also be constricting and frustrating.

Barbara's ex-husband, for example, cared for her welfare to an extent which soured their relationship, and which even her friends found disturbing. *"He insisted on being with me every minute of the day; he even used to go with me to the hairdresser and then wander about outside till my appointment had finished,"* she recalled. *"I felt less and less like an equal partner in our relationship, and more and more like a doll."*

3. QUALITIES THAT LAST

All right then: what are the qualities that stand a good chance of enduring? What sorts of question can you ask yourself about the partner you have at present – or one you may seek in the future? And what sort of price will you have to pay, to achieve a good relationship, anyway? Will it all be worth the effort?

Let's take the criteria first: the question of enduring qualities. Some of these are relatively straightforward ones, which you've probably considered at some stage – and which are appropriate questions to ask at the beginning of a relationship.

Does this person respond to me in a positive way? Do they have a pleasing personality? Is it probable that my friends will like this person – and be liked by them? Do I find them interesting and likeable *as they are now*?

4. MIRROR IMAGE, OR MISSING HALF?

How similar are we? is a question less frequently asked – but it can be a thought-provoking one. Recognising differences and dealing with them constructively can be very difficult, especially if they challenge or intrude on your view of the world: what's fair, what's right and wrong; what's really important. Claire, a successful magazine publisher in her late thirties, is married to a man with a very different personality to her own, but their underlying world views are very similar. *"I don't think I could bear to live with someone who didn't want to get up and get on with things,"* Claire explained. *"I value Chris's differences because his approach to life seems so amusing and interesting; he's a lateral thinker and I'm much more of a single-track thinker. But we do share a sense of purpose, and that makes approaching our differences much easier for both of us."*

Louise would agree. *"Our similarities aren't what first attracted George and me to each other,"* she explained when talking about her second husband, to whom she's now been happily married for five years. *"In fact, I was attracted by the things about him that seemed* very *different – from me, and from other men I'd known. In some ways, our differences are complementary: his impulsive 'let's do it now!' nature is balanced by my more hesitant and cautious one. But we did discover lots of underlying connections and similarities, especially in our family backgrounds, and I can see that those help our relationship to thrive and strengthen, just as much as the differences."*

D. Questions You Should Have Asked Already – And Still Can

1. Will this person depend on me to make their life work – or are they capable of separate growth as an individual? Do they have a happily independent identity, as well as the one they share with me as part of our 'coupleness'?

2. Is this person good at talking about their feelings – or at least, willing to try? Do they listen when I talk, and make me feel that I'm being heard and understood? Are they comfortable about expressing affection? Do they bottle up anger, or do they express it and try to deal with it?

3. Is this someone who likes to receive as well as to give? And to give, as well as to receive? Can this person ask for what they need, and support me in my needs?

4. Do we have enough in common to build a life together that would be mutually enjoyable? Can we respect and value each other's values, even if they are very different?

5. Do we have compatible sexual needs and

desires? Do we enjoy the same expressions of our sexuality?

6. Have we talked about plans for the future together – for example, about having children? Are our expectations of the important 'landmarks' of life similar – and if they are not similar, have we worked out a satisfying compromise?

7. And finally – do I like this person, as well as love them? Do they like me, too?

As a relationship progresses it's perfectly possible to discover that the partner you saw as one sort of person early in the relationship has turned out to be quite another. But if you are clever as well as fortunate, you will end up with a partner who meets your needs as well as your desires, and with a solid foundation on which to continue to build a lasting relationship.

E. But Will It Be Worth All The Effort?

At this stage of your life, it's also quite possible that you are wondering whether it's all really worthwhile. Maybe you've gone through a particularly painful split-up, or perhaps you are finding the day-to-day difficulties of your present relationship especially hard to deal with.

1. WHAT PRICE WILL YOU HAVE TO PAY?

There is certainly a price to be paid for having a relationship – just as there is a price to be paid for *not* having one at all. People don't tend to advise others simply to "get on with it" these days, whatever the cost: that's just not a fashionable school of thought in the enlightened nineties, filled as they are with working women and their financial ability to abandon unsatisfactory relationships. There is, however, a germ of sense at the heart of the "just grit your teeth" advice. It is inevitable that there will be some important level of difficulty in any relationship. It may not be possible to predict what the exact difficulty – or difficulties – will be, but they will most certainly exist.

2. WHEN IS THE PRICE TOO HIGH?

Sometimes, the price can be intolerably high, but the identification of what is an unpayable price remains a uniquely individual matter. Only you can set the limits for your own life: what's certain is that there need to be some.

I'd put the loss of integrity and dignity on my own list of unpayable prices, along with any kind of physical or mental viciousness: probably, most of us would do so, at least in theory. Gordon, a divorced man in his early fifties, would add easy lies to that list: he long ago decided that *"the first lie I'm told in a relationship will be the last I tolerate,"* while Sue, a forty-nine-year-old twice-married researcher, would put public disharmony – rowing and nagging criticisms, and the putting down of one or each other in front of other people – very high on her list.

For Jan, a doctor in her early forties, the idea of a price isn't relevant. *"Almost any couple has reached the point – at some stage in their relationship – of looking at the other person and thinking 'I really don't want to be with you any more.' But we've always managed (so far!) to end any major argument or disagreement with the thought that yes, this is what we want; this is* who *we want, rather than anything or anyone else."*

And Claire doesn't really believe that she's had to pay a high price at all, for her relationship with Chris. *"I've led a much more interesting life, and I've done far more and far better in my career, than I think I could have done outside of this relationship,"* she said. *"Without Chris's unquestioning assumptions about my abilities, I don't think* I'd *ever have questioned my own rather limited ambitions."*

3. KNOWING WHAT MATTERS

Learning to identify what's *really* important to you and your partner will help you to sort out your feelings about the relationship: sometimes, your fears of what will happen if you lose a point, or a battle, or a principle, turn out to be groundless.

"I know I can be very stubborn," admitted Louise, *"and that's been useful in my work – but it's* not *very useful in arguments with George, because I tend to lose sight of the point, and just carry on rigidly determined to prove I'm right, no matter what the consequences. It*

wasn't until we broke up for a few months a couple of years ago that I had time to think through what the relationship cost me as well as gave me, and how I could work out – and maintain – a comfortable balance about all that. I had to be sure that I really wanted a relationship with George at all, before I could decide that I wanted to work at making it a good one."

4. IS THIS WHAT YOU WANTED?

For some people, that's the crux at issue: do you really want to have a relationship? If you do, I believe you'll have to accept that it's never easy; that it will have to be worked at; that you will have to make sacrifices of time and energy and privacy and space and freedom. (If you decide you *don't* want a relationship at all, there will be a price to pay for that, too, but the sacrifices will be different ones. In each case, the rewards of achieving a situation which works well for you are considerable; in each case, the price is a real issue.)

The building bricks of loving commitment depend on your keeping a keen sense of your own identity, alongside a flexible sense of your own importance. We've all seen men and women whose own identity has become almost entirely subsumed into the larger identity of coupledom; we all know people who refer all thought and decision to their 'other half'; we all know people whose unhappiness within a particular partnership is matched only by their fear of separation.

The commitment of a stable and continuing relationship can feed our best characteristics, and our most loving selves. *"I think one of the reasons I continue to love George as much as I do is that I am – without my own conscious choice – a much better person because of his love,"* Louise told me. *"It makes me nicer to be loved by him."*

Perhaps all the adjustments and compromises are, simply, easier for some people, on whose shoulders the burden of commitment rests more comfortably than for other people. But perhaps, too, the truth lies with Eileen's comment. *"Maybe,"* she suggested, *"a successful couple is like two old trees that have grown together on a windy hill. Both have two withered sides through standing so close together, but together they make a sturdy clump that withstands extreme conditions much more successfully than either of the trees could have done alone."*

We Can Work It Out

We're not here to see through each other,
but to see each other through.
Gore Vidal

Chapter Two

We Can Work It Out

A. Key Points In Seeing Each Other Through

1. GOOD COMMUNICATION

It's a good idea consciously to set up positive communication paths with your partner, *before* you run into stormy weather. It's much easier to practise good habits when you don't need to rely on them to get you through a bad patch – and practising really will help: maybe in preventing the bad patch from occurring, and certainly in stopping it from getting worse.

This will mean setting aside time each day to talk to each other about something other than trivial domestic details; it will mean practising listening as well as talking; and it will mean responding to what your partner says as openly as possible.

Louise is sure that lack of communication was the main cause of her divorce from her first partner, years before she met her present partner, George.

"Julian and I both really tried, in our ways, to be honest," she recalled. *"But looking back at it now, it's as if we were both so determined to defend our own rights, we didn't even clearly see that the other person had some too. We spent so much time* not *talking about the real problems we had, and getting so stuck in circular arguments about other things, that I think we just wore each other out. We'd had a deep affection for each other in the beginning, but that drowned, with the weight of unrelieved mutual suspicion tied to its neck."*

2. AVOID AUTOMATIC GRIEVANCE BUTTONS

Sometimes, couples fall into patterns of response to each other that have all the hallmarks of a script. Both know their lines all too well, and both resort automatically to the all-too-familiar patterns of exchange and response. Both use up energy they might have put to more positive use, in the often-deadly routines of accusation, familiar defences and responses, and aggrieved self-righteousness. It's as if a button at the back of two puppets has been pushed, and the characters spring to life, go through their paces, and fall back exhausted. We don't mean to do it like that; we don't even see that that's what we're doing, half the time.

Reducing the power of this sort of automatic grievance button needs courage, determination and practice – but it can also transform how you feel about yourself, your partner and your relationship. Sue remembers the first time that she and her second husband David successfully avoided an old, familiar trap of anger and accusation.

"*I don't think either of us had seen that we could behave differently in that circumstance,*" she explained, "*and the discovery was tremendously powerful for us both. It was like peering down into a deep, barbed trap the moment before you fall into it – and then successfully turning away on to safe ground. We never had so much trouble with that situation again, and I was reminded that I could avoid other problems as well – if I only chose to do so in time.*"

3. IDENTIFY THE PROBLEM

Sometimes, the problem with having a problem in a relationship, lies in identifying exactly what the problem is! And if you think *that* sounds a bit daft, just think back for a moment about the times you've argued at cross-purposes with someone (usually your nearest and dearest). Each of you has your own agenda; each of you is determined to prove that you're right; each of you has a sense of grievance, of being misunderstood . . . and unless one of you 'wins', neither feels that the exchange has been satisfactory. Familiar?

Ordinary problems – the very stuff of daily life – can often be sorted out with goodwill on both sides, and a true willingness to share thoughts and feelings. If there are difficulties about money or children (and these are the two most common generalised ones) – or if one of you is bothered by a specific hurt (why did she criticise me so sharply this morning? what made him so late for the special dinner?) then, despite differences of approach, you and your partner stand a good chance of sorting them out through direct discussion.

But mis-identified problems are much more slippery, and cause us a great deal more heartache. So it's here, in particular, that good communication skills need to be introduced, and that you need to engage seriously in an attempt to identify the underlying causes.

4. LOOK ME IN THE EYE AND SAY THAT!

Erica, a teacher in her early forties, is sure that constant communication practice is the key to the successful relationship she achieves with her printer husband, Tom.

"We make sure that – whatever the pressures – we create time to talk to each other every morning. Not just to exchange grunts over coffee, but to look at each other properly, eyeball to eyeball, and to talk *about something. That means that if there's something one of us might be tempted to brood about, or to mis-interpret, it gets cleared up before it's a problem. And it means that we give ourselves a good chance to be united parents for our children, as well. I saw my parents' marriage founder because my mother was too frightened to tackle any real problem, and so she never confronted anything.*

Yet so much of the time, her fears seemed to relate to a misapprehension of an issue; not to a real problem at all."

B. BEING A GOOD COMMUNICATOR

1. HEARING AND LISTENING

The key to good communication is four-fold. You need:

1. to be able to identify your real feelings; and
2. to be able to say exactly what those feelings are; and
3. to be able to listen to what your partner says; and you need
4. to be able to accept your partner's feelings, even if they are very different from your own.

A good communicator sends clear, direct messages – not ones that are so oblique the receiver needs a code-book to interpret them! When you talk about your feelings, you identify them. If you need something from your partner, you say so, directly. And you also say what you don't want – you don't go along with plans simply to avoid trouble, because you know that in the long run, that will cause more trouble than it avoids. (Few of us, after all, are such good actors that we successfully conceal our feelings about plans we don't want to share – or at any rate, we don't successfully conceal them for long! So the true message – that we don't *really* want to go to Bob's for lunch on Sunday, say – is conveyed to our partner in an oblique way in any case, and overlays any attempt we fondly imagine we're making to indulge our partner's wishes.)

2. DON'T LET ME GUESS – TELL ME

A good communicator receives, as well as sends, messages clearly. You don't just guess what your partner means: if you're unsure you check; if you listen, you don't interrupt to offer solutions or advice. You make it clear that you care about what's said, and that you're really trying to understand. And you avoid second-guessing your partner – deciding in advance for them what they must, or will, mean to do or say.

Second-guessing is a habit we fall into as a relationship progresses and matures, and as you become more confident in your understanding and knowledge of the other person. In a sense, some level of predictability is probably inevitable, as well as pleasing – and there's at least one TV game show which depends on the accurate prediction of your partner's wishes and behaviour, in order to win points. But second-guessing feeds a neglect of what's *really* being said: for, if you already think you know what your partner feels, you'll tend to hear a reflection of that, no matter what the evidence to the contrary may be. And because second-guessing is generally based on what you would want to hear, or want to be true, in a particular situation, it often leads you both down the wrong paths.

3. HAVE THE COURAGE TO KNOW WHAT YOU FEEL

Identifying your real feelings can be hard: it certainly requires courage. The middle of a furious argument with your partner is *not* a good time to try; it's better to wait for a little time alone, and then to look behind your anger or resentment, to the underlying cause. That can be frightening – especially if you fear precipitating worse troubles, or even the end of the relationship, through a truthful examination of what's going on.

But giving fear such power is to give yourself no chance at all, and condemns you to a future surrendered to the power of unexamined emotion, uncontrolled and inexplicable highs and lows of happiness and grief, and the certainty of the problems remaining to cause future trouble. If you dare to be truthful – first with yourself, and then with your partner – you stand a good chance of winning some real power away from the fear, and awarding it to yourself.

You might try planning a time and place to talk things through with your partner – the 'booking' focuses your attention on the task, and agreeing the details on when and where is a good beginning.

Or you might start by writing down the things you and your partner have problems about, and which bother you. Robin, a gym instructor now in her fifties, tried that a few years ago, and found it surprisingly helpful. *"It wasn't the things themselves,"* she explained, *"but when I looked at them and thought about them, I began to see what they represented to me. For instance, it used to drive me crazy when Brian left the bath mat soaked through, when the rest of the family still had to have their showers – and when I thought he could easily have dried off a bit in the shower stall. In fact, that problem had a simple solution – these days there are* two *bath mats; one for Brian and one for the rest of the family – but to be honest, it only got to me because it was a sort of symbol of a deeper and more difficult problem for us: about home responsibilities, and how we shared those between us. It was the big one we needed to tackle, and once we started listening to each other about that, the bath mat was easy!"*

4. HAVE THE COURAGE TO SAY WHAT YOU FEEL

The next step is to express your feelings: clearly and calmly, taking responsibility for how you feel; taking yourself seriously.

There's no point in getting this far and then spoiling the whole thing by prefacing your discussion with "I know this sounds silly, but . . ." or by couching the whole thing in diffidence and apology. Be firm with yourself! Sarah, a solicitor in her early forties, found that it helped her to begin with a little private self-directed pep-talk to raise her motivation level and steel her courage – and to make herself express her feelings calmly and articulately – before she confronted a problem with her partner.

Sarah also finds that writing things down is a useful tool – although that once went amusingly wrong for her, when she'd scripted an especially tricky conversation she wanted to have with a lover, over the telephone. She left her 'script' by the living room telephone – and then answered the call in her bedroom!

Again, pick your moment. Don't choose a time late at night when you're both tired: almost no disagreement or difficulty is as stressful (or insoluble) in morning light as it was the night before. Don't start when you're likely to be interrupted by other people or events. Don't do it when you've had a glass too many (or when your partner has). But – do do it.

5. LISTENING IN

Just as you are unlikely to be able to tell the truth about your feelings unless you feel you can trust the listener, so too with your partner. Good listeners are not born: they're made through conscious practice, and you can become one. It's hardest when you are hearing things you don't like – when you ache for reassurance that it's not really *that* bad, or when you long to change someone's mind, or to correct a fact or impression.

But if you put your own thoughts and feelings to one side, you'll do better at understanding what your partner feels. The feelings may well not be like your own: your partner is a different person, not an extension of you. So you wouldn't feel like that, in response to such-and-such a situation? So what? It's not your turn. Resist any impulse to comment on what you hear, and don't indulge yourself in offering opinions, either. Sometimes you might need to ask for clarification: ask your partner to put something another way if you find it especially difficult to understand, or ask for an example.

Respect your partner's right to have the feelings they do. We can learn to control what we do about them, but we cannot control whether or not we have the feelings in the first place. Trying to understand someone else's point of view can be hard work, and it often involves you in uncomfortable feelings of uncertainty, and lack of control. If you can accept that, then giving your partner space to express *their* feelings will come a little more easily.

C. The Stumbling Blocks To Good Communication

1. FEELINGS FROM THE PAST

When Louise lost her job, George was very supportive and loving towards her – and very encouraging of her attempts to find another one. But after a few weeks, he began to find her continuing unhappiness very difficult to live with. George couldn't imagine why Louise didn't just pull herself together and get on with things, instead of spending time feeling hurt and resentful about what had happened to her – and he began to feel angry as well as irritated, when he found his suggestions and advice resisted. One evening everything came to a head in an explosion of rage on his part – and of fear and resentment on hers. Both of them felt entirely justified in their positions, and intolerant of the other: both believed they knew exactly how they *really* felt.

Pretty soon after that Louise found a new job, and life returned to a more-or-less normal state. But when, a year later, they explored their feelings about another matter with a counsellor, the feelings which related to that old episode began to emerge. George had completely forgotten how his mother's depressions had frightened him when he was small: the 'child within' George, however, had not forgotten, and was terrified by Louise's lowered state. And Louise saw that she had needed a different response from George to the one she'd received – although she'd not realised that at the time, and so hadn't been able to ask. She had wanted an acknowledgement of the pain she felt, and to feel that she was supported and attended to in her present situation, rather than being swamped with advice and suggested solutions. The lack of attention to how she really felt had left her as emotionally bruised and sad as *she'd* been as a child, ignored by both parents for large parts of her young life.

Childhood experience plays a much stronger role in determining adult behaviour than we mostly admit or want to acknowledge: especially in intimate adult relationships. In particular, it seems, our ability to trust the loving-kindness and goodwill of those on whom we depend – our partners now; our parents then – is heavily influenced by our first experiences.

Louise and George's experiences are interesting for a number of reasons. The hidden underlying problems were the immediate cause of the difficulty between them – but that didn't stop the couple from finding other ways to make amends for the argument, and to get on with their lives together. Neither of them understood at the time just what was informing their feelings and actions – and both now believe that the understanding they've achieved, deepens and strengthens their relationship.

2. WINNING THE BATTLE AND LOSING THE WAR

The famous psychologist Dorothy Rowe recently summarised a central point about confrontational arguments between family members as "Do you value pride more than love? Would you rather be right than happy?" And, some years ago, the newspaper columnist Katherine Whitehorn made a related point in an article about relationships when she said that successfully enduring ones were sustained by the three things you *didn't* say every day.

Ms Whitehorn didn't mean that we should avoid saying things like "Thankyou" or "I love you"; rather, that avoiding critical or argumentative stands was a positive action. And Dr Rowe didn't mean that we should give up our own ideas for the sake of peace; merely that winning an argument is not necessarily the point we *really* want to reach. After all, although we may feel and behave as though we long to gain the high moral ground of being 'right', we will discover it to be a very lonely place to inhabit in splendid isolation.

A recent Canadian study which interviewed couples, suggested that disputes between the partners in the survey were mostly seen by them as initiated by the wives (62%) against 25% by husbands. However, the wives 'won' only 25% of the arguments, while the husbands 'won' 64% of them. But what did the winning and losing really represent for any of the couples? Did 'winning' just mean marching out of the room, or getting what was wanted by bullying: did 'initiating' merely involve mentioning that a problem existed, or was there real, active antagonism or nagging involved? Sometimes, there's a lot of wood to get through before the trees can be seen, let alone accurately identified – and the search stands a better chance of succeeding if a confrontational style is avoided.

3. AN INTOLERANCE OF DIFFERENCE

But let's suppose that you've managed to identify your feelings, and to communicate successfully with your partner about a problem – but that the problem isn't the sort that's going to shift easily. Perhaps the characteristic your partner exhibits that drives you crazy is a deeply entrenched part of their nature – maybe it's the flip side of some characteristic you love and admire in them. (For example, Chris's levels of disorganisation would drive Claire crazy, if she didn't realise they're part of the very lateral thinking which delights and amuses her.) The truth is, that's how they are. The characteristic you so object to, is part and parcel of the nature of your partner. It's unrealistic to expect change. What can you do about *that*?

Just tolerating someone else's difference can be very difficult, especially if you're a confident and assertive person, used to getting – and holding – your own way in most things. You just *know* your way of doing something, or of dealing with something, is the best way: why on earth can't your partner see it that way too? Life would be so much simpler . . .

And so would life be if you lived with a Ken or a Barbie doll, but it wouldn't be half as interesting! However similar you and your partner may be – let alone how different – the individual remains an entirely separate being, to at least some extent unknowable to any other individual. What's it worth to you, this discomfort about your partner's habit? Is it worth a discussion, to see if it could be adapted or altered – or if understanding might help you to relax a little and accept it more readily? Is it worth an argument; a flexing of will – a power struggle to establish whose rights and need should dominate in this relationship? Is it worth forfeiting the relationship altogether?

Well, the answer depends on you. If you simply hanker after an ideal of perfection, you'd be wise to consider giving up the idea of an enduring relationship with another human being. If you've lost sight of the fact that you, too, have habits which your partner finds at least equally stressful, then you might just try the simple exercise of exchanging lists of 'what I love' and 'what I dislike' with each other: ten positive ones, five negative ones, and brace yourself for the latter!

It's also possible that some of your important needs are not being met by your present partner. If that is the case, you will have to decide what to do about that. Can the needs be met in other ways? Can a discussion of the needs reveal a solution you hadn't seen? Do you need to revise your idea of the future? You won't know the answers to any of these questions, however, unless and until you've worked through some serious attempts at communication – at sharing your loving feelings as well as your unhappiness and anxieties; at communicating respect and affection as well as disagreement.

4. THE INABILITY TO SAY 'SORRY'

The world did not need the line from *Love Story* – bestselling book and blockbuster movie of the mid seventies – which told us that loving someone meant "never having to say you're sorry". The implication was that your lover knows how you feel without having to be told: apologies, however, like the people themselves, should never be taken for granted. Loving someone means that you *often* have to say you're sorry.

If you're one of those people who finds it very hard to get your mouth around the words of an apology, you'll probably do a lot to avoid making one – but a bit of practice helps, and so does a careful choice of words with which you can be comfortable. For example, saying "I'm sorry you feel so miserable" instead of "I'm sorry I upset you" keeps the responsibility for feelings with the person who's having them, yet it is sympathetically aimed at the heart of the matter. The right words really can help.

For others, apologising is easy enough – perhaps even a mite too easy. If the words trip with such facile ease off your tongue are you sure you really mean them? And try to guard against using "I'm sorry, but . . ." which is sometimes just an introduction to a list of more grievances, rather than a genuine attempt at reconciliation.

D. A Change Of Heart

The truth is that love hurts, and a civilised and generous approach to your partner feeds your best instincts and the positive things between you. The good manners of life – the pleases and thank-yous, the good humour and the smiles – are an absolute essential in relationships.

Sue, in particular, said she relied on these to get her through the bloody-minded moments of life. "*I fall back on behaving as if I felt loving, or enthusiastic, or kind, in the moments when I feel anything but – because I know it's just a blip in my moods, and I don't want that to wreck everything.*" And this attitude highlights the importance of choosing the kind of communication you and your partner should seek to emphasize between the two of you.

1. COMMUNICATE THE POSITIVE

It can be dangerously easy to communicate negative feelings – but the real point of good communication is to transmit *positive* feelings to each other: it is these which establish, nuture and sustain a good relationship.

One counsellor likens this process to opening a savings account in a bank. The currency of the account is the feelings which the couple have towards each other, and the deposits are made by the expression of goodwill, affinity and closeness. The withdrawals, on the other hand, are made by expressions of ill-will.

The stronger the feelings and its expression, the larger is the deposit or the withdrawal. And it won't do simply to avoid expressing a feeling, either: feeling bad and saying nothing about it still makes a withdrawal from the 'relationship account', while having good (though unspoken) thoughts also makes an inevitable deposit.

That analogy demonstrates how it's possible to build up a credit balance of goodwill – and how it's possible to bankrupt the relationship. You might consider how this works for you and your partner. Which of you makes more deposits of goodwill, or do you both contribute more or less equally? And do you both make negative withdrawals? Can you think of ways to increase the deposits, and eliminate the withdrawals?

2. CHOOSING A STATE OF MIND

Feeling angry or happy; feeling hopeful or depressed; feeling high- or low-spirited: these are all states of mind which operate in powerful ways on our lives. Each one of these has, for each of us, characteristic thoughts and actions which accompany it. When your spirits are up and you feel good about life and everything in it, you tend to behave in certain ways, and to say certain sorts of things in response to the day's happenings, or in response to your partner's demands and desire. When you're down and depressed, your perception is very different: and so is your behaviour.

And the point of all this is suitably simple. If you learn to recognise your moods, to mistrust negative states of mind, and to choose to concentrate on positive ones instead, your relationship will benefit.

Sarah remembers a lunch with her mother years ago, when they were both fascinated by watching an older couple at another table. "*They were having such an animated conversation,"* Sarah said. *"They were filled with an enjoyment of each other; they radiated positive feelings throughout the restaurant! I've always thought they were a perfect example of a loving perspective on life. It looked like a marvellously balanced relationship, which satisfied them both. And I've always thought my mother was a little envious of what we saw that day: she and my father had a successful relationship, but that was more because she gave in to him at every turn, than because they shared such an intimate common ground of happiness."*

3. COPING WITH MOODS

Everytime your mood shifts, you experience a new perspective – a different view of reality. Like all of life's habits, your moods establish patterns, and while it isn't sensible to try to force yourself (or your partner) to change the mood you're in, it is wise to acknowledge its effects, and to wait for a bad mood to shift before you take important decisions. Feeling depressed, for instance, contaminates your thinking: everything is coloured by gloom and despondency. You need to be able to identify the mood, see past it, and do your best to keep your spirits up whilst waiting for your mood to change. When your partner is in a low state of mind, you need to learn to put their behaviour in that context. Don't hold a mood against yourself, or against your partner.

"When Louise feels low, the whole world knows it!" explained George. *"If I let that get to me, I'd be sucked into a lot of depressing conversations about our relationship and Louise's ideas about the problems in it. But the black thoughts and worries move away with her change of mood: they don't have any reality outside the moods, which is something we both understand now. I can cope with that, in fact it's never bothered me much on my own account: that's just how she is, and I know to leave her alone until she comes out of it. But I am sympathetic – at least, I hope I am! Because it can't be much fun, being in the grip of such gloomy thoughts."*

How To Have An Argument

I was angry with my friend:
I told my wrath, my wrath did end.

William Blake

Chapter 3

How To Have An Argument

A. The Inevitable Highs And Lows

1. ACCEPTING IMPERFECTIONS

In every intimate relationship that endures through time, some tensions and difficulties will eventually surface. After a while, however idyllic the beginning has been, an occasional boredom or irritation with your partner begins to surface; or some external pressure interrupts your satisfaction with each other. Sometimes the difficulties are more dramatic, and felt more acutely; sometimes they develop over long periods of time. The only certainty is that they will arrive – and that they will deserve (and in any case, often demand) attention.

Unless you are still engaged in a romantic desire for perfection, you'll probably be able to acknowledge the inevitability of some highs and lows occurring –

and to accept a few imperfections that you couldn't see in your partner before, suddenly coming into a sharp and unforgiving focus. But the issue remains of exactly how best to tackle the problems, once they have surfaced.

2. SHOULD YOU JUST CONCENTRATE ON THE GOOD THINGS?

Some people decide – through intention or default – to do nothing at all direct about problems in relationships. Just put up with it, their advice would go – count your blessings instead. Or think of what your partner puts up with in you. Or concentrate on what's good about your partner, and just get along by ignoring the difficulties.

This attitude can serve well for the minor irritations of daily life. Carol, for example, thinks that accepting the whole person who is your partner is the key to happiness in day-to-day dealings. *"It's not like picking over goods in a shop,"* she points out. *"You can't say I'll have this aspect, but not that one! If, instead, you remind yourself – well, I've chosen this person and I'll concentrate on the good things about them, it creates a useful habit of mind for sticky moments."*

In some cases, however, the advice doesn't apply so effectively or easily: situations, like people, change and develop – and what might have seemed fine at one time – or at least theoretically endurable – becomes impossible to bear in another context. Sylvia, now in her late fifties, had an easy and affectionate relationship with her husband until he retired – and then she suddenly found his constant presence around the house in the daytime dreadfully oppressive.

No amount of gritting her teeth solved the problem: Sylvia felt that her space had been invaded, and badly needed to regain the balance between shared and private time, which they had achieved before. In the end, the solution she found was a part-time cleaning job which provided an alternative 'private space' for her to inhabit for a few hours a day, and the relationship resumed its normal course. But Sylvia now appreciates the importance for her of some time alone, and knows she must preserve that for herself.

3. WHAT ABOUT THE OBLIQUE APPROACH?

Of course, Sylvia solved her problem without discussing it openly with her husband – mostly because he was already feeling off-balance because of taking early retirement, and she didn't want to exacerbate his problems by making him feel unwelcome at home, too. But discussion was also avoided because Sylvia and her husband have formed the *habit* of doing so: in their relationship, problems are solved obliquely and indirectly, or they are simply endured.

In part, this is both a generational and a cultural point: it hasn't long been part of British expectations of social behaviour that we should openly and directly confront problems in relationships – and so we have a much stronger history in avoidance techniques, than we do in open talk as a method of problem-solving. As long as committed relationships were based at least in part on necessity – so if you *had* to put up with what you'd got, you might as well do so in a positive frame of mind – it made good sense to advocate gritting your teeth in any circumstance.

But the age of working women and mid-Atlantic psychological trends have transformed those expectations, and long-term relationships are more likely to be caught in a trap between an ideal of romantic love, and the pressures of two high-powered working lives, than in wildly-differing role expectations. Indeed, problems now may be as likely to be talked *into* existence, than never discussed at all – for you can, of course, create and enlarge problems by some methods of approaching them, and the over-dramatisation of difficulties can be as troubling as not acknowledging them at all.

4. HOW IMPORTANT IS IT, ANYWAY?

Even if tackling problems by avoiding or ignoring them can't be taken as a serious approach, we shouldn't throw the baby out with the bathwater. Assessing the *relative* importance of a problem is an essential step on the road to dealing with it – and some problems just don't thrive in the light of day, or under close inspection.

How many times have you been tempted to begin an argument late at night, over an issue which seems utterly essential to happiness – but in the morning can no longer remember why the issue seemed so important? How many times have you found that when your sense of humour has unexpectedly intervened in an argument, your perspective has equally suddenly shifted away from taking yourself and your rights so self-importantly?

Helen, a music teacher now thirty-four, has been married to Peter for ten years, and thinks that their senses of humour are the most important tools they use in finding ways through problems. "*Laughing is the best diffuser of tension between us,*" she said. "*I think that if you can laugh together, everything else will more or less take care of itself. When I can see the funny side of something, I can generally find a way to cope with it.*" And Sue often finds that an argument with David ends, not because the issue has been resolved, but because neither of them can remember what the point was supposed to be. "*It's as though we have a sort of hiccup in our force field, or enter a Bermuda Triangle of communication,*" she said, "*but then it's over, and it's as if we never had the cause in the first place.*"

"*I have quite a lot of trouble with my own shifts of*

perspective," admitted Joan. *"It's as though I put a template over the situation, that only lets through evidence which agrees with what I've already decided. So, for instance, if Danny does something that I think is controlling, I can have him mentally hanged, drawn and quartered for a lifetime of merciless control of me and my freedom, before I've even worked out how to talk to him about it. That means that I often approach the problem in a very combative mood, which escalates what could have been a straightforward discussion into a battle of wills."*

5. GETTING AT THE TRUTH

Some difficulties do ebb and flow with time, and those are the ones which seem to respond best to a reflective approach. Try tracing the problem back, not only through your present relationship but also back through earlier life. Do the feelings that you have about it remind you of earlier feelings, or of other situations? It's often the case that an earlier anxiety or set of responses has been triggered by this new situation, and it's the earlier ones which are feeding the present. Once you understand what's causing your response, you can begin to tackle that, rather than blame your present situation or your current partner for your own past history.

Other difficulties tend to dominate and intrude on the well-being of the relationship, and the happiness of those within it: they demand attention, and the pain of denying or ignoring them can be exhausting, and debilitating. You can submerge yourself in work or distractions; you can continue to behave as though nothing is wrong – and then something apparently quite unrelated occurs, and all your self-control evaporates in an explosion quite out of proportion to the situation: an explosion which has little to do with the matter in hand – and everything to do with the denied and ignored truth.

Louise remembers this problem from her first marriage, to Julian. She and her husband were unable to resolve their difficulties, but social and economic pressures kept them together as an apparently stable and happy domestic unit for several more years. "*There were times when I could forget what was wrong – in fact, I could forget that anything was wrong at all,*" Louise admits. "*But then something would happen – maybe we'd spend time with an affectionate couple whose commitment to each other was plain for all to see, or Julian would go off by himself for days at a time, or make it clear he didn't value what I thought or felt – and I'd feel as though I was drowning in pain and fear. Denial was a lot more destructive for me than publicising the truth could ever have been."*

Often, too, we may hesitate to confront a problem in a relationship because we lack practice in dealing openly with emotional issues – or because the experiences we've had in attempting to do that have been bad ones. Or it may be fear of the consequences of confrontation: of losing control through expressing anger; or of losing your partner's love through revealing unattractive sides of your nature such as jealousy. Fears like these are powerful and controlling ones, and dealing with them can be both difficult and painful. Talking them through with a friend or counsellor can reduce their power – and the admission of their existence to your partner can be an enormous relief.

6. WHAT ANGER CONCEALS

Anger is a bit like pain – it's an indicator that

something needs attention. Sometimes we use anger as a mask – and as long as we shout, rage, and accuse others of various sins, we conceal from them – and often, from ourselves – something we fear: perhaps that their love has vanished, or that we don't deserve it. Such fears usually have their roots in childhood experiences: being able to acknowledge them to ourselves, and to talk about them to others, helps to remind us that we are grownups now, able to accept our history, accommodate its difficulties, and put it to work for us. But domestic rows can be appallingly painful experiences for both partners, and leave them shaken for days afterwards, wondering just how they are to deal with the storm of feelings which has been unleashed.

This is probably one of the main reasons why so many people try to avoid rows at all costs – but that's not realistic behaviour, if we want to seek long-term solutions. The price we pay for avoiding the row is often high in both mental and physical ways, through stress-related illness. And in any case, the anger *does* express itself, more often than not, in some way – and so most of us end up doing just what we thought we'd avoided!

B. The Right Reasons For Arguing

1. TAKING A POSITIVE APPROACH

In fact, it can be an excellent idea to argue with your partner. Not a no-holds-barred row – a focused argument. Not one conducted in violence or with shrieks of rage: but in a constructive exchange of truth. Not one filled with expressions of bitterness, or with outpourings of repressed resentments: but one informed by a genuine desire to improve or modify a situation, or to clarify it, or to express your feelings about it.

2. ACKNOWLEDGING THE FEELINGS

In our culture, to suggest that you should seek out arguments, rather than avoid them at all costs, could sound like madness. ("We *never* argue!" is the sort of couple-claim which is often accompanied by especially smug expressions.) The same often seems to be true of expressing feelings – whatever lip service we pay to that, we believe at bottom that feelings are dangerous things, and should be kept firmly in control by the application of logical argument. Because anger is such a powerful force, many people fear argument: the rush of negative emotions, the destructive energy they experience. All the couples I interviewed for this book admitted to having arguments – but, significantly, all had developed techniques for dealing either with the arguing itself, or with the aftermath of disagreement.

"We use arguments to clear the air from time to time," said Claire, *"but we always make sure that we stick to the subject that's bugging one of us, and we always try to let that subject run its course. I'll probably try quite hard to avoid an argument in the first place, but when they are over and the subject is sorted out, I feel tons better – much more positive and relaxed."*

3. REDUCING TENSION

Well, it's certainly sensible to avoid some sorts of argument – the kind that increase tension rather than dispel it. And the sort that are really just an excuse for a shouting match, or for a bit of bullying, aren't much use, either. But constructive arguments really do significantly reduce tensions, and do a lot to increase feelings of closeness, and genuine intimacy. So consider these basic rules about fighting fairly; taking responsibility for your own feelings; and using the conflict to improve and enhance your relationship.

C. How To Have A Constructive Argument

1. TAKE THE RISK

If you're one of the many who argue with their partner only in their head, and almost never commit themselves to the real thing – think about why. Does this help you to nurture and sustain a sense of grievance? Are you able in this way always to keep your partner in the wrong? Have you decided what your partner will say, think and feel, and does this give you a sense of moral superiority?

None of these strategies is a good investment in the future of the relationship. In one sense, they are symptoms of an exercise in control, and of attempts to feed the victim in you. Of course, we often wish that our partners could guess what's wrong without our having to commit ourselves to the danger of a direct expression of our feelings – but it's far more likely that the guess won't be made, or that it won't be accurate.

2. BE SPECIFIC

Try to avoid instant analysis and interpretation of why a certain behaviour is being expressed by your partner; just concentrate on the behaviour itself. So, for example, "you always try to control me" isn't centred on any example, and begs for an unhelpful blocking reply like "oh no I don't!" Try a specific example, like "I feel unhappy when you make all the decisions about where we're going to go and then tell me what we're going to do. I'd like to share more of that with you, and feel more in control of my own life. So I'd like to discuss the ideas with you before any decisions are made."

3. STAY OFF THE OFFENSIVE

It's very easy to attack your partner when you'e irritated or angry, or when you feel threatened or wronged – *but it doesn't help to argue in those terms*. Sentences that begin "you make me . . ." or "you always . . ." or "you never . . ." encourage the other person to be defensive against the attack, rather than to attend to the message. If this happens they are more likely to concentrate on protecting themselves against you, rather than to open up to the possibility of change.

On the other hand, if you start your sentences with "I feel that . . ." you stand a much better chance of getting through. Trying to make your partner responsible for your feelings, however, is another dead-end. Taking responsibility for the way you feel – but giving responsibility to the relationship to help you turn the feelings around – is harder, and takes practice, but it's a lot more effective.

Remember, too, not to engage in personal attacks. If you feel cornered or begin to panic, deal with *that*: don't use the red herring of how fat your partner has got recently, or taunt them with some private, privileged knowledge you know will hurt them. Such bullying tactics may shut down an argument, but they will do nothing to increase understanding, respect or love.

4. GET TO THE POINT

Lots of couples spend massive amounts of time and emotional energy arguing about relatively trivial issues – like Robin and Brian with the wet bath mat. The more difficult and emotionally loaded the real issue is, the greater is the temptation to allow a trivial one to take its place: in the cool light of rational assessment, matters which would scarcely raise your eyebrow, let alone an argument, carry an extraordinary weight of drama and significance. The issues aren't that important, it's true – but *something* is that important to the couple in question – and that something, or things, is what badly needs to be addressed. The more quickly you can uncover the real matters and deal directly with them, the better your relationship will be – and the less emotional power will attach itself to the subject.

5. BE HONEST ABOUT YOUR FEELINGS

If there's strong emotion attached to an issue – and in close relationships that's almost always the case – it doesn't help to behave as if that's not true.

Stripping a confrontation of its emotional content might seem like a 'polite' or a 'controlled' way to handle it, but it's more important to get the feelings out into the open; to acknowledge them as real; to allow them space and importance. Without that happening, the feelings can't be dealt with, and they'll continue to trip you up. We often deny that we're angry, for instance: to ourselves as well as to others. "I'm not angry, just sad." Well, maybe you *should* be angry – and maybe you really are, too.

6. DON'T LIVE IN THE PAST

We often sabotage our partners' efforts to change – or our own – by attaching credibility only to past history. "I've always been that way" isn't a justification for what *should* be – after all, you could always try things a different way – and "I know you've said you're sorry and you'll change, but I'll never forget how awful you were last week/month/year when you did such and such" is as destructive to the partner who's choosing the role of victim, as it is to the one being nagged.

7. DON'T THROW THE KITCHEN SINK

If you're feeling very resentful or angry about something your partner has done (or neglected to do) don't make a discussion of that an excuse to mention every grievance you've felt for the last six months! "And not only that . . .", "While I'm on the subject . . ."; "And what about the time when . . ." "Come to think of it . . ." roll off your tongue all too easily, and not only is the original issue lost; your partner's chance of a positive response is drowned in a sea of criticism. The same thing happens with sweeping condemnations: "you're impossible/completely aggressive/absolutely incapable/hopelessly stupid" makes certain that your partner won't be in the mood to take your points seriously: either they'll be too defensive to listen; or they'll have shut down their potential sympathy in preparation for battle.

8. DON'T USE THE SILENT TREATMENT

The trouble with the silent treatment – where one partner withdraws communication, and sulks, refusing to speak to the other for hours and even days at a time, as 'punishment' for a fault – is that it doesn't correct or change the point of conflict. Sulking, in fact, is a sort of oblique expression of anger – and it's cheating your partner to express anger in this way, as well as cheating yourself of a clear expression of your unhappiness.

9. DON'T GIVE UP

Don't run away from an argument, or stop in the middle of it, or change the subject when it gets too hard to confront, or leave the issues unresolved – or at least unreduced. If it all becomes acrimonious and shows signs of turning into a violently expressed rage, then you must close it down as quietly and responsibly as you can – but if you find yourself, the day after an argument, going over and over the conversation in your head continuing or improving on the exchanges – then it's not over. If you are still angry or resentful towards your partner, you haven't finished.

Of course, if something interrupts you before you've finished, like the arrival of guests for dinner, you'll have to wait until they've gone – but try to reach a point at least of reduced tension before you finish; somewhere where it's possible to feel comfortable and caring about your partner (and they with you) before you stop. But don't force the disagreement to remain beyond its natural life, either! If the issue has genuinely lost its significance, or if you just can't remember what the point was, don't hound it to death: find something positive to say instead.

10. DON'T HOLD FORTH, OR BE A NAG

Going on and on about something that you want to change (or want changed on your behalf) is a common habit – and just as common amongst men as women, whatever the folklore tells us! But repetition won't help change your partner's mind, nor engage their attention if they've 'switched off'. You'll need to revise *your* behaviour, if you want theirs to change.

Louise and George's counsellor taught them a standard technique which they have found very useful in dealing with the expression of strong emotions between them. Each of them takes turns to make their point about how they feel – and then the other partner rephrases what's been said, before continuing their response to the point made, or before stating their own feelings. The first partner then, in turn, rephrases the points made to *them*, before replying.

"We've found this has a number of advantages for us, and it's helped a lot," agrees George. *"You do have to listen to each other carefully, in order to make sure you understand what's being said. It slows down the whole process to a speed at which it's much easier to be clear and specific, and much harder to interrupt, or bully, or lose your temper."* And Louise says that both of them find it very soothing to hear their feelings 'affirmed' by repetition – not agreed with, necessarily, but accepted as a true record.

D. Arguments To Avoid

The emotions we feel do not necessarily offer us an accurate picture of the world around us: they reflect aspects of ourselves. The information that an emotional response provides is not external information about our lives and our partners: it is internal information about the person feeling the emotion. And sometimes, unquestioned emotions can lead you into having the sort of arguments that would be better avoided.

1. THE SELF-JUSTIFYING FIGHT

If you feel anger towards your partner, you naturally think that they did something to justify your anger. They may have done – but the anger describes you, not them. If you feel dissastifised with your relationship, you're bound to think there's something wrong with it. That may be true: it may also be false: the dissatisfaction doesn't prove it, either way. The truth is, you may be wrong – or, rather, your feelings may not be an accurate reflection of what's going on.

You need to be sure that the 'script' you follow is honest and your own; the one you freely choose – not just the one you were given by your parents, for example. The emotions we grow up with seem like reality to us – if your parents showed a lot of anger, then anger is likely to have become a big part of life for you, too. But it doesn't *have* to be that way – and it won't help your relationship if you have acquired the habit of automatically choosing to express negative emotions. So do be sure that the argument you want to have, is about an identifiable reality that properly belongs to the two of you.

2. A MIND-SET OF MISTRUST

Everyone tends towards a habit of mind in response to certain situations. "There's nothing either good or bad, but thinking makes it so" is a piece of Shakespearian wisdom which is often helpful to remember when you are trying to sort out emotional conflict.

Anything we spend a lot of time thinking about can easily become a mind-set – as anyone who's tried to diet knows. The more encouragement there is to think about food (the meal you've just had, the one you will have next, the one you wish you could have right now, the snack you're allowed to look forward to and the one you know you mustn't have) the hungrier you become, and the more obsessed with eating.

In one seminar for troubled relationship held in the States, the participants were asked to think about any particular relationships they were engaged in with another person. If, deep down, they truly believed they had tried their best to do right by the other person, they were asked to raise a hand: every one of the one hundred people present held up a hand.

Then the participants were asked to consider how they felt about the other person in the relationship. Did they believe that this other person truly had their best interests at heart, too: that they were trying as hard as they could? Less than a third of the participants lifted their hands.

If you don't believe your partner has your best interests at heart: if you don't think they mean well, and you can't give them the benefit of the doubt – then an argument won't help. You will need to deal with the mis-trust first.

3. THE HABIT OF NEGATIVITY

"Peter and I once tried an experiment where we were deliberately sweet and nice to each other for a whole day," related Helen. *"We chose to say only positive things, no matter what happened. No shouts, no*

grumps, no complaints of any kind. It reminded me just how petty most of my grievances are, and how often I seemed to take pleasure in expressing dissatisfaction. Peter's resentments felt the same to him. It was strange, because we cleared away a lot of potential argument material, but we did it by not expressing anything."

It's worth stopping to wonder if you jump into an argument with, perhaps, just a touch too much enthusiasm! You might try the Helen and Peter experiment if you suspect that's the case, or if you find yourselves starting off too many days on the wrong foot with each other. Sorting out problems is fine and good – but sustaining a habit of intolerance is quite another matter.

The Dynamics Of Change

Love is what you've been through with someone.
James Thurber

Chapter Four

The Dynamics Of Change

A. Ambivalent Attitudes To Change

1. RELYING ON THE PAST

People's attitudes to change in any form tend to be, at best, ambivalent – and never more so, than when personal relationships are the issue. "But I've *always* done it like this!" is a cry from the heart, which resounds throughout the adjustment period of any new living arrangements! This appeal to the past – to tradition – is one of the most powerful available to us, carrying as it does not only the assertion that we have things exactly right as they are, thank you, but also the accompanying and underlying implication that if change is called for, it's going to have to come from somewhere other than ourselves.

2. LOVE ME, LOVE MY HABITS

The habits that we have accumulated so far in life serve us in a number of ways: some simple, some complicated. Some of the habits have obvious practical advantages; others resonate with messages from past lives, or represent a level of unexamined, automatic response to situations. But all of the habits have one thing in common: our attachment to them as part of our personality.

And of course this is a large part of the reason why it's much more difficult to adjust to the new routines of a live-in relationship in your late thirties or forties, than in your late twenties. Our personalities have become more formed; more certainly shaped by then, and so we have accumulated habits – of thought, of action, of routine – that we enjoy and make us feel good. We are unlikely to take kindly to someone wanting things to be different.

Kate, an insurance director, found this especially hard in her late thirties, when she married Luke. *"I fell madly in love with him – I think a sort of combination of fantastic sex and admiration of his talents as an artist – but that didn't stand a chance once we were together. I hadn't realised how important my domestic routines, and especially my peace and quiet, had become to me – and Luke just ripped all that apart. He was noisy and messy, he had noisy and messy friends who arrived at all hours and expected to sit and drink with him; he mixed his oil paints on anything to hand, including my best china; he left his clothes in heaps all over the house. And he didn't want to discuss any of that as a potential problem – he thought I was just being boringly middle-class and making a fuss over nothing important. Good sex and great art just weren't enough in opposition to that, though I admit they might have been when I was younger."* The marriage lasted only a few years – and Kate has never shared her home with another man, although she has had several satisfying and successful relationships since splitting up with Luke.

3. SHARING ROUTINES AND SORTING OUT ROLES

One of the minor – but nonetheless satisfying – delights of a newly intimate relationship lies in forming the basis of a set of routines and patterns, as a couple. Sunday mornings take on a special new pleasure as you enjoy establishing the way in which you'll spend that free time together, and habits are formed in affectionate and loving harmony: reading bits from the newspapers to each other over breakfast, sorting out the washing before lunch, catching up on shopping for supermarket staples in the afternoon: all signs of the establishment of routines which we cherish, and in which we indulge.

But the very same delights can turn sour with habitual use, or become chores that one person is left to do because the job must be done – instead of two people sharing it because they want to be together. It isn't that you *want* your response to these shared intimacies to change: they have simply done so. And the barriers you have jointly and lovingly constructed against the world's interference, can also become the bars of a prison.

Let's suppose you've always done the weekly food shopping. At first, you enjoyed the task of shopping for two, but lately you have begun to feel hard-done-by as you slog around the supermarket aisles on Friday nights; resentful as you pack everything into cartons at the checkout in a grim race with the checkout staff; a sad victim of unfair circumstance as you heave the cartons into the boot of the car – and unbearably put-upon as you lug the cartons out of the car again, and into the kitchen at the other end. You put everything away, you stack the cartons and packaging neatly outside – and then, filled with silent rage and a fine sense of moral outrage on your own behalf, you decide you've had enough. *Things are going to change!*

But when you ask your partner to share the weekly shopping jobs with you, she refuses.

Now, maybe what you'd most like is that the shopping could be done by both of you together – but perhaps you'd be happy with a compromise, such as – alternating the shopping week by week, or splitting the tasks up from one go at the supermarket to smaller shopping expeditions. But how are you going to get there? How do you start to ask for change?

The same problem can arise with systems you establish between you that have a deeper significance. For example, one of you might be the one who always makes holiday arrangements, or does the gardening, or plans redecorations. Agreements like this are often established early in relationships, and as long as both partners are comfortable with the situation, they will take root and form part of the structure of daily life.

But what if one of you develops your own interest in gardening? Or begins to want an involvement in picking holiday destinations? Or suddenly decides to assert their taste over the living room carpet? An alteration of this kind can really rock the boat of the relationship, if it challenges the unspoken (and maybe unconsidered) balance of power for the couple. And since most people have large amounts of happiness, self-awareness and comfort invested in the position they hold in relation to others – their power – this is likely to be a sensitive matter.

4. WHOSE TURN IS IT?

Perhaps the best relationships are those in which control and power are shared in a way that gratifies the needs of both people. If this happens amicably, or spontaneously, you may never be consciously aware that responsibilities have been shared out like that. If one of the two of you wants to do the cooking, say, and the other doesn't – then fine. If your partner enjoys DIY and you are happy to go along with whatever wallpaper or storage systems are chosen: great.

The trouble begins when the apparent acceder turns like the proverbial worm and displays a real need either to share, or to take turns – or when through a natural process of change and development, the needs of one of the partnership actually alter. If the resulting changes are not asked for by the one who wants the change, or not surrendered deliberately by the one who would have to change, there's often a sort of underground power struggle which develops, and which can continue through shifts in circumstances and ground, for as long as the relationship lasts.

"My first husband thought of me as a domestic servant," remembered Sue. *"I was always the one who did all the cleaning and cooking and child-care and sorting out of our daily lives: he did nothing at all of that. I don't blame him for taking up the offers I doubtless made in the early days of our marriage, but I do wonder why he continued to exploit his position throughout so many attempts on my part to change things*

just a little. Things had to change – and in the end, his complete immovability caused the rift between us which led to our divorce."

Maybe the most important point to remember in all of this, is that change is, simply, inevitable. It's part of life, whatever we choose or however we try to delay or to control the way in which changes affect our lives. And since it *is* inevitable, participating in the process at least allows you a way of affecting the outcome.

"Marriage is not a conscious change, but a series of small adjustments," said Eileen. *"I don't really think that a relationship can last unless it's capable of change, but you can realise changes* have *happened and respond to that knowledge, rather than engineering them in a deliberate way."*

Helen feels that her relationship with Peter has changed out of all recognition since they were married – *"and it's all for the better, too! We have become entirely comfortable with each other – in fact, I feel as though I've grown up with him, which I suppose I have, in a way. We have a very companionable relationship now, but I started off by seeing Peter as a very different person to the one I now share my life with*

– much less sensitive and vulnerable than he actually is. One of us has changed – but most probably, we both have: I in the way I see him; he in the way he is with me. At any rate, we now make a very good team."

B. Negotiating For Change

1. THE DIFFICULTIES OF BEING ASKED, OR ASKING, FOR CHANGE

Asking for change – or being asked for it – in a relationship is a process of negotiation. If you don't like the way your partner is doing something, you're going to have to enter into a process of negotiation to effect change. If you can, jointly, find a way to agree on a definition of what's wrong, and if you are both able to talk freely about what you want to have happen in response to that, you have a good chance of achieving a resolution to the problem that both of you will be able to accept, feel comfortable about, and live with happily. You can both feel that you've won.

The ideas of success and failure; winning and losing; are not ones which translate their values appropriately to a personal relationship – but we often have great difficulty in *not* attaching competitive standards to what goes on between us. In itself, this arena is one of negotation too – but it's all carried out at a much more subtle level.

2. AVOIDANCE TECHNIQUES TO GUARD AGAINST

We may punish our partners by withholding affection, or sex, or both: by silent disapproval, as well as by angry words of accusation. If the disputes over change become prominent and constantly unproductive, however, they can seriously damage your sense of self-worth. The issue of control is rather like a sort of third party in a relationship: where, although the superficial discussion turns on plans for a holiday, the underlying and undiscussed reality turns on who is going to get their way: the issue is of who's in charge.

C. If You Are Being Asked To Change

It's worth taking time to sort out your response: you're much more likely to end up with something you feel comfortable about if you do. Sharing your anxieties with your partner might seem difficult – but investing in the trust that's involved in that, is important to you both.

1. DON'T ALLOW YOURSELF TO BE RUSHED INTO DECISIONS

Take them in stages, especially if you feel frightened of the very idea of change. And if you do feel frightened, it will help to try to face your fear, and to work out what this represents for you. What's the worst that could happen? What's the best? What would be a comfortable compromise for you?

2. IDENTIFY THE SPECIFICS OF THE REQUEST

Think as clearly as you can, about the specifics of what's being asked for by your partner: panic will only cloud the issues and prevent you from being able to assess them. Have there ever been other situations in your life where change seemed dangerous and threatening – and is the memory of those colouring the present?

3. LISTEN AS CAREFULLY AS YOU CAN

Make sure you are listening to what your partner is actually saying: don't assume before you hear. Ask for clarification and specific detail if you aren't sure what's meant. Don't assume that you're under attack, or being unfairly criticised: try to remember how hard it is to begin such a discussion, and stick with responding to the initiative as fairly and straightforwardly as you can.

"I have always had trouble accepting criticism from Brian," admitted Robin. *"I think it was because my father had always nagged on and on at me about*

anything that didn't meet his exacting standards, and so I was mentally braced against that happening. It takes a lot of trust to let someone say what they want changed, and it was hard for me to see that it wasn't me *that was under attack; just a habit of mine that made Brian feel bad."*

4. TRY MAKING A COUNTER-OFFER

If what's being asked isn't acceptable to you, don't just leave your partner with a bleak refusal. Show that you can respond with courtesy and respect to their proposal, even if you can't agree with it. Sometimes, just the acknowledgement of the other's needs can help relax the situation between you, and lead to a genuine exploration of other possibilities.

5. STICK WITH THE NEGOTIATION AS A TWO-WAY PROCESS

Don't give up on the process easily or quickly: stay with the discussion as long as you need to. Modify your counter-offer if it's not acceptable. If the process makes you feel anxious or defensive, offer to think things through and respond at a later time, rather than just refusing to continue, or turning the situation into a competition to see which of you can be the more stubborn.

6. DON'T GET SIDE-TRACKED

This is *not* the moment for a counter-attack, so resist the temptation to trot out all the things that *you* want changed about your partner, even if you feel threatened by what's being said.

D. IF YOU ARE ASKING FOR CHANGE

1. THINK OUT WHAT YOU WANT IN SPECIFIC TERMS

Be as direct as possible about your requests. It won't do, for example, just to say you want to be more of an equal partner in the relationship: you'll have to be able to spell out the specifics of the new situation you're seeking. If you haven't worked out what those are, and thought out what you need, the discussion won't end up where you want it.

If your request refers to something smaller – like a habit of speech, for example, to which you don't respond well – you will need to be both specific and exact. And it will be better to do all this sooner, rather than later. Discovering that you have *always* felt uncomfortable about being called 'sweetie pie duckling' in public or private, but have taken two years to pluck up the courage to ask for an alternative endearment, can be much more distressing because of the time lapse, than it would otherwise have seemed!

2. EXPLAIN YOUR REQUESTS CLEARLY AND THOUGHTFULLY

Explain your requests to your partner in clear terms, and use as much tact and thoughtfulness as you can. Don't be angry when you make the request, and don't decide the battle can't be won before you've even begun it. You may well be resentful or hurt or confused, but those are *your* feelings, remember: your partner is not responsible for them. Don't begin the asking-for-change process whilst you're locked into a state of mind which characterises you as the hard-done-by victim, and your partner as the exploitative baddy.

"*I easily fly off the handle,*" explained Helen, "*but if I want Peter to consider changing the way he does something, I know that confrontation from me in that state is the last thing that will do it! So I try, now, to wait for a good moment, and then to explain exactly why I think an alternative strategy would be better. For instance, Peter's a terrific father, but we used to disagree quite a lot about disciplining Jamie, until I sorted out a way to suggest changing how we dealt with him – separately and together. Now Jamie knows where he is with both of us, so he's more sure of himself – and he can't exploit the old difference he used to sense in our approach to him.*"

3. CLARIFY YOUR REQUESTS

If your partner seems not to understand what you want, don't retreat into anger or sulking or despair, or assume that your request has been rejected, just because you haven't immediately achieved what you want. Maybe you could make it clearer – are you sure you aren't concealing the request a little, in an effort to test the waters on its acceptability?

We often have a great deal of trouble listening to (and hearing) what's being said in emotionally-loaded situations – and however good you think you are at listening, it's quite probable that you mis-hear, or mis-interpret, what's said to you some of the time.

"I used to get enraged when it seemed as though George heard the exact opposite of what I said," Louise told me. *"I thought he was doing it on purpose. It never occurred to me that underneath that cool, controlled exterior he was in as much of a panic as I was – but expressing it differently. We've learned to take discussions much more slowly and calmly now, and to make sure we listen – and hear – the other person's views. But it took time and practice to get it right."*

4. BE PREPARED TO MODIFY YOUR PROPOSAL

Be prepared to do this before you begin, and don't lose your temper, or sight of your goal, because you don't get exactly what you have asked for. Don't mistake winning, for getting what you want – they're seldom the same thing!

Let's suppose that you've both decided to have people to supper, and your partner wants to ask her old friend Dizzy to come. The trouble is, you don't like Dizzy at all: you find her boring, her conversation is repetitive, and she's the last person you want to have sitting at your dinner table for an entire evening. Your partner generally sees Dizzy when she's out with the girls, and so you've never had to admit how much you dislike her, before. What can you do?

One possibility is not to say anything: but then Dizzy will come, and will most certainly get on your nerves – and one way or another, the evening won't be much fun for *you*. But if you decide to try to negotiate a change in the arrangements, you discover that asking Dizzy to the party is very important to your partner: Dizzy's been a supportive and close friend for ages, and just can't be passed over as easily as you would wish. Without Dizzy, the evening won't be much fun for your partner.

The best way through this will be some form of compromise. You might decide that it doesn't matter all that much if you have to put up with Dizzy just for an evening from time to time – if she's so important to your partner, maybe you can work on your nerves! (But in this case you really should share your feelings about Dizzy with your partner – *not* so that you earn lots of Brownie points for your noble endurance, but so that your Dizzy contact-time is limited in the future.) Or you might have a drinks party instead of a supper party – so more people will be able to be invited, and Dizzy will be diffused for you in the general chatter, yet available to your partner.

It will help if, in advance, you've worked out some alternatives which would help, and if you persist both in offering these, and in your efforts to explain why it's an important issue for you.

5. DON'T GET SIDE-TRACKED

If you allow your partner to distract you from your purpose by countering your requests, you'll find it harder to begin another set of requests any other time. Stay with your need until you have reached a conclusion you're happy with: don't be tempted to follow a red herring about other unshared tasks or other resentments. This is *your turn*: don't let it be sabotaged.

E. You Win, I Win Too

Confronting an issue squarely is one thing. But if you confront your partner as an adversary in negotiation, and decide that since only one of you can win, one of you has to lose – and by God! it won't be you – you will probably ensure that you get nowhere, uncomfortably. You dig in your heels and refuse to budge: so does your partner. You take a position on the nearest high moral ground, and your partner responds by trying to turn the whole thing into a joke. Or sulks. Or simply feels miserable, confused and misunderstood. What have you really won?

It is possible for you to find a solution together which incorporates 'wins' for both of you – but you'll have to start from a different viewpoint than the lofty, and solitary, high ground! If you see your partner as a collaborator in the effort to achieve happiness for you both, and if you're willing to look at a range of ways this might be achieved, you stand a good chance of having two winners in the room.

CRISES AND TURNING POINTS

Where is it now, the glory and the dream?
Wordsworth

Chapter Five

CRISES AND TURNING POINTS

A. ACCEPTING THE INEVITABLE

Even the happiest of couples go through times of crisis – times of dramatic change, when suddenly they are faced with a specific difficulty which means they must re-evaluate their life, and their relationship, and how these things fit together.

No crisis automatically means the end of a relationship. Whether or not the relationship survives depends on the two of you, not on the crisis itself. Relationships are as resilient as the people in them, and there are no rules that say that *this* is allowable; *that* is not. But the new situation created in response to the crisis *will* mean that – weathered or not – your relationship will never be exactly the same. What happens next depends on how you feel about the crisis, and what you do about it together.

B. THE COMMON CAUSES

Undoubtedly, the main causes of crises in relationships are usually related to problems with money, children, or sex. These days, crises are often triggered by external causes like unemployment or redundancy – or by some other difficulty related to employment or money matters which precipitates an emotional as well as a practical reassessment within the relationship. Or perhaps it's that most infamous of all crises for couples – the affair: maybe you have discovered that your partner's seeing someone else, or maybe you're the one involved in another sexual relationship. Or an unplanned pregnancy might introduce the necessity for a choice to be made which, in the ideal world of theoretical planning, wasn't scheduled for some years to come.

1. WITHIN THE FAMILY

Sometimes an external crisis like the death of a parent can trigger a further crisis between you and your partner, because the new situation throws old problems and unresolved matters between you, into a fresh and sharper focus. Amongst people I know, the death of a parent has been the immediate 'cause' of two people leaving their partners: those involved have felt liberated from some sort of unfinished business with parental disapproval, and finally free to do things they know the dead parent would have deprecated. And difficulties with the children of a partnership, especially when (as with teenage children working through rebellious periods, or with older children leaving home and also leaving their parents' relationship exposed) these create conflict between the parents, are another classic case.

Issues related to family roles are frequently disruptive and confusing ones in our lives, if only because they arrive bedecked with baggage from other, earlier lives – our childhoods, or our previous relationships. It can be hard to unravel all that, identify the hidden meanings and respond intelligently – whilst also trying to cope with the day-to-day repercussions which the new circumstances have sprung on you.

Anna, now thirty-seven, has been married to Martin for eleven years, and described a recent crisis between them, when Martin's constant absences from home threw all the family responsibilities on her shoulders.

"I was nailed down by domestic duties and isolated from adult companionship – and the pressures on me felt relentless. But we didn't seem to be able to discuss what was wrong, and it was that which actually triggered the crisis – not the situation itself. I felt like a single parent with non-stop responsibilities; Martin thought that I was just trying to make him feel guilty about needing to be away for his job. He understood in the end, but not until I'd had a minor breakdown, which shocked us both into solving the problems, together. *And now that we're on the other side of all that, we are much clearer about ourselves, and what we expect from each other. We had a breathing space when I went away for a few weeks, and that brought back the good things between us; now I'm learning to drive so I can be more mobile and get to classes. And Martin has taken on a bit more responsibility for family matters, too."*

2. THE EMOTIONAL PRICE OF LOSING YOUR JOB

The practical problems which relate to loss of employment are profound ones, but their emotional aspects – such as the loss of a daily structure, of status and self-value – are just as significant as the loss of income, and just as difficult to deal with.

John lost his job as a computer analyst two years ago – and it took him seven months to find alternative employment. He spent most of that time, he now says, in 'a swirl' of misery and self-doubt. *"I really understood those men who pretend to their wives that nothing's wrong, and leave home at the same time each day to sit for hours in the park or the library,"* he said later, with a rueful smile. *"I didn't do that – but there were often times when I wished I didn't have to confront how I felt. I'm grateful to Sally now for her support, but at the time I did wish we could pretend it hadn't happened!"*

3. JUST DRIFTING APART

Communication practice can be an essential tool to put to use in successful crisis-resolution, and getting methods of discussion, disagreement and compromise sorted out between you beforehand will help enormously. Jean and Danny experienced a sort of non-specific crisis in their relationship, after about four years together. Danny had changed his job, and worked much longer hours; Jean's mother was ill, and she spent more time visiting her parents in a nearby town than she had before. These alterations in their lives brought tensions for the couple, as their previous casually-achieved closeness disappeared, and new understandings had to be forged between them – and to be reached by deliberate discussion, for the first time in their life together.

"Every time we reached a point of disagreement over the way we might reschedule our time together, I could see Danny beginning to panic," said Jean. *"He'd had a very rigid upbringing, where emotional issues were never acknowledged, let alone discussed, and he just seemed to lack the language to express his feelings. His reactions varied wildly from retreat into hurt silence, to enraged*

attacks on me – all of which made him as unhappy as it made me! Only a counsellor helped us to identify what was going on, and only lots of practice for us both helped Danny to develop other more positive methods of response."

C. WORK OUT WHAT YOU WANT

Working out what you genuinely want can be difficult when it's entirely possible to want two conflicting things at once, as well as to want things that aren't available to you! And it's hard just because facing a crisis takes courage, at a time when your personal resources already seem stretched thin. But unless you do look it straight in the eye and decide to explore and resolve it, its power over your life will continue to grow, and to poison any good things remaining between you and your partner.

D. CONFRONT IT TOGETHER

Erica and Tom are sure that the key lies in regarding such problems as belonging to the couple, and not simply to one or the other person, together with an underlying assumption that you *are* going to work it out, whatever it may be.

1. A PROBLEM FOR THE PARTNERSHIP

Erica explained. *"With an immediate cause of distress for your partner, like unemployment, this might mean that you need to listen a lot – maybe to boring lengths – through the depressions and moods which arise in consequence, and which may create rifts if they don't get attention. The problem is not just yours, and not just your partner's: it's a problem that the family firm – the partnership – needs to tackle. I find it perplexing when I observe an unwillingness to be supportive in difficulties, in one or other of a couple: it's as though they think sharing and helping only happens in the good times."*

2. IT'S ALL *YOUR* FAULT

Erica's comments make sound advice, although it will be easier to follow when the crisis is caused by an emotionally less-threatening issue such as unemployment, rather than, say, an affair. But it's certain that assigning blame is never helpful, and if you do it you will also slow down any process of healing or reconciliation. So try not to spend time blaming each other – or blaming yourself – for what's happened. Instead, use the time in more constructive ways, such as in identifying and expressing your feelings.

3. A PUBLIC MATTER

Any crisis will be exacerbated – sometimes unbearably so – by its becoming newsworthy. The loss of privacy can throw an intolerable burden on the couple, and delay – or destroy – the chances of finding a shared way forward.

One stressed marriage which *has* survived the glare of publicity is that of Kevin and Pandora Maxwell. After the death of her now infamous father-in-law and the collapse of the family-run business, Pandora's husband Kevin became Britain's biggest bankrupt, with debts of more than £400 million. In a recent newspaper interview, however, Pandora made it clear that abandoning her husband had never been an option for her.

"People have said what a star I am because I'm still

here with Kevin. It's extraordinary, because in many ways I think it's strengthened our relationship, because he has been more dependent upon me in the last year than he probably was in the past. It's important to him that we're all here and functioning and going on."

E. A Crisis Of Fidelity

Again, however, it may well be harder to keep anything functioning, or make any process towards resolution, when the problem is one of sexual or emotional fidelity.

1. THE ETERNAL TRIANGLE

Most of the people I interviewed for this book thought of an affair as *the* potential problem within a relationship – although many would also have agreed with Eileen when she pointed out that it was really a symptom of some other problem, rather than a prime cause in itself – and with Claire when she said that there were many worse things for couples to do to each other.

Many relationships survive one or both partners

establishing additional sexual or close emotional ties with 'outsiders', but the undoubted pain of discovering the existence of a secret, separate world your partner is inhabiting, as well as – or in opposition to – the one you share together, can be devastating. What do they do together? What do they share that you are excluded from? Do they talk about you?

2. THE GREEN-EYED MONSTER

Jealousy – and a shattering sense of betrayal – are the almost-inevitable results of discovery, which can surprise you with the force of their passion. Three hundred and fifty years ago Francis Bacon said that excess passion was "like a short madness", and the idea of a 'mad passion' remains in our language as a description of feelings apparently beyond our control.

"Our marriage has survived my husband's affair," one woman said, *"and in some ways we work better as a couple than we used to – we talk more, for one thing. But I don't think I'll ever be able to forgive him for the anguish he caused me. It still hurts to think about it,*

three years later. I suppose I'm impressed that I could survive feeling so betrayed, and still have any loving feelings left for him. I never mention it: it's a pact between us not to do so. And I know he's terribly sorry he caused me so much pain. But still, I long for the day when being reminded of her and how he felt about her, doesn't make me feel sick."

"At first, I was so jealous of the other man I wanted to kill him – or both of them – or even myself," admitted Keith, a married man in his late thirties. *"I didn't feel sane, and I didn't care what I did or said. It wasn't until grief took over that I began to want to sort out what had gone wrong."*

There's no way to avoid the necessity for talk about the causes, if a way forward is to be found. At first, the shock may make you feel too hurt or angry or bewildered to think clearly: you'll need time to think, and time to sort out your tangled emotions. Quite often, the first overwhelming response is rejection – of the idea of your partner's behaviour, or of your partner. Trying to work out what has caused the affair may just seem too painful to contemplate.

3. IN THE PUBLIC EYE

As if all that isn't bad enough, imagine how it might feel if you had to endure the private pain against a background of national publicity and intense media interest. One woman to whom I talked, whose twenty-year marriage was recently threatened (although in the end not destroyed) by her husband's affair with a much younger woman, remembers the alarming experience of being 'doorstepped' by photographers and reporters the morning after her husband had left home.

"I think it could quite literally drive some people round the bend," she told me. *"Having to put on one face to the press and deal with the real matter at another time and in another way was deeply painful and very disconnecting: I felt as though I was at least two separate people. It slowed down our efforts to talk to each other, and it put my feelings on ice for months. Then, as soon as I thought it was safe to have feelings again, they simply overwhelmed me: all that unfinished business and repressed emotion completely swamped me."*

F. EXAMINING THE REASONS

In Keith's case, his wife had begun an affair with a friend – partly in protest at Keith's apparent lack of sexual interest in her, and partly as a delayed response to the death of her older brother: the man she chose as a sexual partner had been her brother's best friend, and the two had become emotionally close through their roles as joint executors of her brother's estate. But the reasons can vary greatly.

1. A PASSING DESIRE – OR SOMETHING MORE?

An affair can signal a passing desire – a one-night stand, for example, which happens in never-to-be repeated circumstances, and which probably owes more to some flickering moment of sexual excitement, than to a genuine problem between you and your partner. In this case the incident may mean little or nothing to the one who's had the affair, but it may still be of great importance to their partner, if it's discovered.

An affair may also represent an important rift in

your sexual harmony, or in your emotional closeness. Helen was very close to having an affair a few summers ago, when she and Peter had temporarily lost the close intimacy of their life together. Peter seemed never to be at home, and when he was, seemed too engaged in his work to 'be there' for his family. *"I tried to explain what was wrong,"* Helen said, *"but I don't think Peter heard. He certainly doesn't know just how close I came to having an affair with Andrew"* (the handsome pianist she met at summer school) *"or how delicious it was to feel like a fourteen-year-old again."* Helen worked her way through the situation, talked some of it through with Peter; decided not to risk her marriage – and then used an imminent family holiday to re-establish a closeness with her husband.

An affair need not represent an ending, but it may be that which is being signalled. If one or both of you have moved on from the shared understandings which kept you close, the immediate result can be unfaithfulness. It's as though, as Eileen described it, *"the shoe isn't fitting you any more, and you decide that this is where it's pinching."*

2. HAVING A BIT ON THE SIDE

All this assumes that you and your partner have a sexually exclusive relationship in the first place. None of the couples to whom I spoke thought that intimacy and trust could be built in other circumstances: they all put faithfulness high on the list of important 'given' understandings.

Marriage – the western world's most usual version of pair-bonding – is certainly a cultural universal, which predominates in every society in the world. Monogamy is more culturally specific than marriage: and most societies allow men more than one wife – but even so, it seems that most of the time, humans tend to prefer to have one spouse at a time.

Adultery, however, is a different matter. Kinsey concluded, in the 1950s, that about half of all American men, and about a quarter of all American women, were unfaithful to their partners at some time during their marriage. There's been no survey since then that can be accurately matched to the Kinsey Report, but related ones in the 1970s and 1980s suggest a dramatic increase in the percentages of unfaithfulness. If those surveyed are telling the truth, an awful lot of us are spending a great deal of time deceiving our partners in other people's bedrooms.

Certainly, some men and women find that a continuing sexual expression outside their primary relationship is exciting and fulfilling, and the adrenalin rush of that excitement is addictive for them. It makes them feel special – more attractive and more desirable.

"We are very discreet, and take great care that our partners will never find out," said one woman in a recent anonymous letter to a national newspaper. *"I have been married for 27 years, had children when I was quite young, spent ten years at home bringing them up, retrained, and now have a good job. But having had sex with only one man, I began to wonder what it would be like with someone else . . . For me, it is a way of having some of the freedom I never had, having been brought up with the idea that I was destined to be a wife and mother, and nothing else."*

3. NO DISCOVERY, NO DAMAGE DONE?

If your partner *never* finds out and so you avoid causing them conscious pain, maybe there's no problem? Well, maybe not: but are you *sure* you're not withholding something as well as the knowledge? Something important to your growth as a couple? And can you really prevent the 'finding out' from happening?

"I discovered that everyone knew except me!" is one familiar cry – and so is "But surely he knows?" A situation in which one partner does indeed 'know' but pretends they do not – from fear; for the sake of keeping the peace – is one filled with unsatisfactory communication, as well, perhaps, as unsatisfactory sex. Is that acceptable between the two of you? Only you can decide.

G. How To Cope As The 'Wronged' Party

1. As you begin to try to respond to the anger, fear and grief you feel, you will probably want to blame your partner for the situation. It will help to see the

problem as one shared by both of you – for blaming is a dead-end street, with only a transitory satisfaction. This can be the hardest acknowledgement to make, but also the most useful. It will be easier to achieve that, if you start by expressing the emotions you feel – however strong, however apparently destructive. A counsellor can help, and so can a good friend. But there are various techniques to try with your partner, too, to help both of you reach a joint understanding and to look sensibly at the future.

2. Remember that talking to a trusted friend eases a lot of the pain – but the talk really needs to take place with your partner. Don't use a friend instead: use them as well.

3. Ask yourself – how can I talk through my feelings clearly and helpfully? How can I find a way to re-establish trust? How can I find a way to mend my damaged pride, and re-establish my sense of self-worth?

4. Ask yourself, and ask your partner, what you both want for the future. Don't dwell for too long in the past unhappiness: do acknowledge it, but do move on from it too.

5. Try to find the answer to *why*, and – if you want to re-establish the relationship with your partner – see if you could help that 'why' to change. Here's where counselling can be invaluable: together, you can discover what's happened from both your points of view, safely explore your partner's feelings as well as your own, and perhaps begin to regenerate some goodwill.

H. HOW TO COPE AS THE 'GUILTY' PARTY

1. If you are the one having an affair, you'll need to work out whether that's because you're signalling your wish to leave the present relationship, or whether your message is about unhappiness with something within the relationship, to which you're nevertheless still committed. All of this needs to be worked through with your partner, before you'll be able to move on: either within the same relationship, or outside it, to a different life.

2. Ask yourself: Am I trying to avoid looking at an existing problem with my partner? What is missing from our relationship to make me available to others?

3. Did you *want* to 'get caught'? Sometimes, people use outside sexual experiences as an indirect way of signalling their unhappiness about unrelated problems within their present relationship. If you leave such blatant clues as to make discovery by your partner inevitable, you may well be forcing your partner to take responsibility for a confrontation you lacked the courage to initiate yourself. If your affair was some sort of plea for help to patch up a damaged relationship, or if it is filling a gap in intimacy, you and your partner need to look beyond the affair, at what you have together.

4. Do you lack faith in your partner's ability to respond to your needs, to care about them, or to change their own behaviour? If that's the case, maybe it's attention you seek – or increased levels of communication. Having the courage to discuss any of those matters with your partner, rather than engaging in the transitory 'displacement activity' of an affair, would be hard: but it might also be worth the effort.

5. Are there other satisfactory ways of proving that you are personally attractive, or just of

finding adequate distraction from tension or boredom?

I. Choosing A Positive Way Forward

1. IDENTIFY THE CHOICES

"You do have choices in this situation, however much you feel trapped and frightened," points out Robin. *"The trick is to look for long-term as well as short-term ways through. That means not getting stuck with feeling guilty or hurt; it means deciding how it would be possible to stay together, or to separate, and then getting on with the consequences of your choices. And that's a good deal easier said than done!"*

Maybe the crisis has revealed sides of your character, or of your partner's, that were previously buried. Sometimes you can discover weaknesses in yourself or others that you wish were not there – but the knowledge is in itself a strength, and you may be able to see the positive side of the new characteristics, too.

2. A NEW KIND OF TRUST

Sometimes, a crisis in a relationship can so badly shake the confidence and trust the partners have in each other, that one or both of them doubts their ability to regain those feelings in the future. Can you be sure the problem won't arise again? Can you really trust your partner and the new understandings and promises that have been made?

If there has been an honest account of what's happened, and a real attempt to seek new understandings, then confidence and trust *can* be regained – but they will be different from before. Trust is a fragile thing, and it can be destroyed: accepting that's true, feeling the sadness of the loss, and then building a different structure will be necessary.

You might ask yourself, however, whether the sort of trust you felt before was a grown-up one, which allowed for human imperfections and errors – or whether your expectations were bound to be betrayed when they were confronted with harsh realities. It's not realistic to trust another person with everything: to trust them to be perfectly (and predictably) reliable is to expect the inhuman of humans.

3. FORGIVING THE IMPERFECTIONS

Of marriage in these circumstances, Bel Mooney's anthology "From This Day Forward" has this to say:

"The slow and painful recognition of imperfection in a partner, and the accommodation of that recognition, will leave a marriage shaken but strengthened. Perhaps recognition comes after an affair, following disgrace in business, or simple low-level crime; . . . all these can be accommodated. Elastic sides of the marriage bond give and stretch in response to the demands placed upon it – almost, but never quite, snapping. The cynic might say that partners 'accommodate' each other because they are afraid of isolation. I prefer to imagine that the 'injured' partner sees weakness and need in the other's face – then peers in the mirror to see the same, turning back to forgive."

The Good Times Are All Gone

When asked why all her marriages failed, Margaret Mead replied, *"I have been married three times, and not one of them was a failure."*

Chapter Six

The Good Times Are All Gone

Everyone reading this sentence has been touched by divorce in some way: by a sister or brother's marriage breakdown; by their parents'; by a close friend's, or by their own. Add to those the breakdown of relationships outside marriage, and we have an astonishingly pervasive picture of the lack of 'ever-after' happiness amongst modern couples. Maybe staying together is a dying art?

A. Untying The Ties That Bind

1. A DIVORCED WAY OF LIFE

There is now more than one divorce for every two new marriages in England and Wales, according to the Office of Population Censuses and Surveys. Since the Divorce Law Reform Act in 1969 removed the need to assign blame to one or other party, divorce has increased by 500%, and Britain tops the European divorce statistics. In the USA, marriages are as likely to end in divorce as in death. And while there are no available statistics for the breakdown of relationships *outside* marriage, it would certainly be safe to assume that there are at least as many or more, even within the group of committed, live-in couples.

In "Anatomy of Love", Helen Fisher collected data on divorce from sixty-two different cultures, which shows a pervasive cross-cultural pattern of decay in marriage. The patterns of human bonding, it seems, regularly show a cluster of divorces after four years of marriage. This seems unrelated to the divorce rate, for it happens in societies where the divorce rate is high, and in those where it's low, or rare. It even remains constant in a society where the rate itself is fluctuating. Maybe, then, there's an inherent weak point in marriages?

2. WHAT'S WRONG WITH THE EXPECTATIONS?

That may be so – and whatever the timing, where unhappy married people can leave each other, they often do. It's clearly a very good thing that they no longer have to stay – for financial or social reasons – in marriages where they find no happiness or joy. On the other hand, there seems to be something badly amiss with our expectations of what should go 'right' in close relationships, or at least of how to achieve the 'rightness' we seek.

What should you do, if things seem to have gone wrong – so wrong, that you want to end it?

B. THE BALANCING ACT OF DECISION-MAKING

The decision whether to separate, or to stay in a relationship, is often painfully complicated by practical circumstances, as well as by emotional issues. You have, after all, got used to things being as they are – even if they're unsatisfactory. You will have property and possessions in common; you may well also have children; you will certainly have opinionated friends and relations: all these make splitting up a time-consuming, laborious and despairingly painful process.

And we know that there will always be bad times

as well as good times: in any relationship; for any couple. So recognising that the balance has permanently shifted from 'enough good bits' to 'too many bad bits' can be harder than you might think.

1. THE POWER OF INERTIA

Since it's also generally easier *not* to do anything – which usually means staying – rather than to take action and upheaval in your stride, and to go, sheer inertia as well as fear can be a factor. Maybe you secretly (or none too secretly) wish that your partner would make the break, and so take the responsibility for decision-making away from you. "I don't want it to be my fault!" you cry, at least temporarily forgetting that since the relationship is a shared thing, so too is any fault in its collapse. 'Fault' is a word best avoided in this context – but the responsibility is certainly there, and so, at least for now, are you. Is that what you want?

2. HOW DO YOU KNOW IT'S OVER?

"I very much wanted to stay in my first marriage," said Louise. *"I fought extremely hard to make it work, and I believed so much in the idea of staying married, that I was grimly determined to hang in there despite the awfulness. I remember that I kept saying I'd not promised to do it if it was easy: I'd just promised to do it. I tried to treat love like an act of will. It wasn't until someone gently suggested to me that, perhaps, the truly loving thing was to stop making demands that my husband no longer wanted to try to meet, that I was able to think about letting go."*

Then again, your good intentions to make the break without rancour or rows may not last as long as packing the first cardboard box. *"When I did finally leave, Julian and I had the biggest row of our relationship over just one book,"* remembered Louise. *"We'd had two copies of it when we married, and after a couple of years Julian had given one of the copies away to a friend of his:* my *copy, as it happened! I simply exploded with rage when I found out: I stood in the living-room shaking with anger. I suppose I was just wound up so tight, anything would have done it."*

Or maybe you begin to leave, and then find it all too dreadful to contemplate, after all. Sue started to run away with her lover (now her second husband, David); lost her nerve at the railway station, and returned just in time to repossess the 'Dear John' letter she'd left on the mantelpiece. (She did finally leave, some months later – because by then she was certain it was right to do so, and doesn't for a moment regret it. But, she now says, *"the earlier moment had been stampeded by my heart, before my head could accept the necessity of dealing out such pain to other people."*)

3. PUTTING IT TO THE TEST

Some couples precipitate a crisis in order to test their relationship: and it's not uncommon for one of a couple (women, in particular, it seems) to file for divorce in an attempt to shake or frighten their partner back into a commitment – or finally to end the pretence of one. Of course, the problem with that technique is obvious: through anger or impatience, or a desire simply to stop the present situation from continuing, you may precipitate something worse, which you may bitterly regret later.

Some of the best advice possible if you're contemplating separation, is to think through the consequences of going – *and* of staying – as clearly, and as fully, as you can. Sarah thinks a list of the pros and cons really helps, and that the list should be a comprehensive and a realistic one. "*Then, spend time imagining life without your partner,*" she advised. "*Get away for a few days if you possibly can, so that the thinking isn't interrupted by domestic trivia. And don't just imagine, for instance, how lovely life would be without the present rows or the insults or the unhappiness: imagine your life* without this person in it. *Look at the far side of the consequences of splitting up: for you, and for the children if you have them.*"

4. FINDING OUT ABOUT LETTING GO

Some people have found a trial separation useful, although the very artificiality of the trial period can be misleading. But one couple who agreed to live apart for a year after going through a difficult period in their relationship, returned to their life together with renewed respect, trust and love for each other. *"I was frightened I'd lose Fiona if she was away for so long,"* said Barry. *"On the other hand, I knew that trying to stop her would be the sure way to lose her forever."* And Fiona discovered that, despite her original doubts, she very much wanted to return to Barry: they married a month after she did so. Few of us, however, have the opportunity – or inclination – for such an experiment.

But there are circumstances in which separation is often the most clear-headed and ultimately loving option available – for example, when your partner is an alcoholic who constantly refuses or reneges on treatment, and as constantly expects your acceptance and support – indeed, your complicity – for their ungoverned behaviour. The concept of 'tough love' acts in opposition to such acceptance and support, and advocates the withdrawal of complicity; the denial of acceptance and support. Saying, in effect, that you will not help someone kill themselves is as tough on the partner, as the one for whom support is denied, and you will need professional advice and counselling to see you through.

C. ACCEPTING THE UNCONVENTIONAL

Perhaps you've discovered that your relationship doesn't match up to your ideas about how it *should* be – or, maybe, to someone else's idea of what a committed relationship involves. If the difference between the ideal and the reality is a constant rub, you may lack the inclination – or perhaps even the courage – to throw convention to the winds.

1. A LONG-DISTANCE LOVE AFFAIR

Kate's experience is a good antidote to this. A high-powered insurance director in her forties, and with the marriage to Luke behind her, Kate has now found great contentment and happiness in a long-distance relationship.

"We see each other every six weeks or so," she explained, *"and it's* always *lovely. We have dinner; we talk non-stop; we make love with undiminished pleasure; we grab time to be together whenever possible over those few days. Then we fill in time between meeting with trans-Atlantic telephone calls. I'm always interested in Ross and what he has to say and what he's*

been doing; he's always concerned and supportive and appreciative of me. There was a time when we thought maybe we wanted more – and we did consider trying to organise our lives so that we could at least live in the same country, a few years ago. But we were smart enough to realise that – for us – that might well not work, and if it didn't, we'd lose what we have now. Why risk spoiling something that's this good, and that we both enjoy, just because it doesn't meet the current idea of togetherness? We might easily not love each other so well, if we had to put up with each other's obsessions and difficulties on a daily basis. Besides, this way Ross'll never have to know just how horribly hairy my legs are – I can time the waxings to match the visits!"

2. EVERY FAMILY'S SECRET

Many close relationships – whether inside or outside the institution of marriage – are unconventional in their structure. Any counsellor who works with couples confirms that the differences in expectation and practice amongst them, are about as diverse and numerous as the actual numbers of couples. Whether you sleep in the same bed, the same room, or even the same house, for example, is as varied an experience as are sexual appetites and practices, and private games. Some couples are married but live happily in separate houses, meeting once a day or once a week; some couples live in the same house but have separate kitchens and separate bedrooms, into which the other is formally invited in spontaneous or pre-arranged ways.

Anything is normal – provided that the people involved are comfortable and happy with the situation, and no-one's rights are infringed. It was Alan Bennett who said something along the lines of "*every family has a secret: its secret is that it isn't like any other family*".

3. WHOSE RELATIONSHIP IS IT?

So, if it's a matter of *difference* that's causing the problem, at least have the courage to pause, and to ask yourself who's having this relationship, anyway? Your mother, your Auntie Paula, the man next door, or you? Sometimes it can take a bit of bottle to do things your way – but none other will do, in the long run.

There was no doubt, for example, of the commitment which Harold Nicholson and Vita Sackville-West had to each other, within one of the best-known unconventional marriages of this century, which survived a number of same-sex passions on both sides. Both thought that marriage "*was only tolerable for people of strong character and independent minds if it were regarded as a lifetime association between intimate friends . . . But . . . husband and wife must strive hard for its success. Each must be subtle enough to mould their character and behaviour to fit the other's, facet to facet, convex to concave.*"

D. WHY MUST IT BE FOREVER?

One counsellor I spoke to said he thought it a mistake to characterise relationships as successful only if they didn't end.

"I can think of one which lasted for twenty-one years – a success, I'd have thought, for both people at the time they were having it. Yet, when it ended, they and their friends were upset about the 'failure'.

"I think it's essential to look at what you have to give away in order to keep a relationship going; sometimes

the price can be a very high one. Why not view a successful relationship as one where two separate people retain their individuality and respect that quality in the other person? I sometimes witness a sort of frenzy in people when disagreement or difference occurs, or when the threat of separation occurs. But should you give away your power and control to keep a relationship going? Or give up your separateness and individuality? Should you stay in a relationship because you'll be lonely without it? I think these are the questions that need the answers."

E. IT'S HAD ITS DAY

Some relationships have a natural, inherent term, and were never intended to be permanent ones. Even if you both enter it with the best of loving intentions, the clash of life-styles, or habits, or ideas of what the relationship will involve, take their toll.

Carol found that her relationship with Alan could survive only as long as no challenge was made to the established structure. *"The moment I asked Alan to consider changes to the way we existed together – what we shared and didn't share; the time we spent together;*

what we talked about, and so on – the whole thing fell apart. Alan liked the relationship how it was and couldn't tolerate the idea of change: I had begun to find it too static and boring. So the difference in our requirements did eventually show, even though it took five years to do so."

F. FORGIVING AND FORGETTING

A friend once told me that, although she and her husband would probably forgive each other anything, they took care to behave as though that wasn't true. They didn't take each other for granted, and they didn't presume on the loving-kindness that each felt for the other. This care and attention for the dignity and well-being of your partner contrasts with the pain brought by personal revelations like the existence of long-term hidden affairs, or by having your own rights and needs completely ignored by unthinking selfishness.

1. DON'T SLIP INTO A SOUR RELATIONSHIP

If you are consumed by jealousy or anger because of your partner's actions, it can be very hard to 'give away' the feeling. You can intend to do so; you can believe that you have: but the feelings can sometimes return unbidden – and before you're aware of it, you are once again consumed by bitterness and grief. The underlying suspicion and lack of trust in such circumstances can, and often does, sour a once-good relationship – and undermine the possibility of reconciliation ever really taking root.

2. THE PROBLEM OF LOST RESPECT

Continuing a relationship filled with bitterness and resentment is no way to live a life; neither is one which doesn't deal honestly with identified problems. It's certainly the case that counselling may help you find a way through the unhappiness to a new and different understanding as a couple. But living with someone for whom you have permanently lost respect seems an impossible double burden, doomed to bring out the very worst in both people.

G. "BUT I CAN'T LET YOU GO!"

It does not please us to see ourselves as dependent, clinging children, unable to countenance the idea of survival away from our parents – and yet the fear of abandonment remains with many adults, and feeds their grown-up relationships as it fed their childhoods. And because the child's fears were so complete – because what was feared was the denial of life, which is after all what the absence of adult protection represents to a young child – the new protector's threatened abandonment brings those responses to the surface once again. But your lover – ex or otherwise – is *not* your parent, and you are no longer the child in fear of abandonment, however much that child's needs insist and intrude on your adult life.

1. ACCEPTING AN ENDING

It's *not* the end of the world – but it is the end of something, and endings can be bitterly painful and lonely times for the people who endure them. Even if you're 'the one who has made the decision' to enforce an ending, you'll probably feel confused and uncertain: about the decision itself, about the memories of the good times; about the future.

2. ACCEPTING A NEW BEGINNING

Again, counselling or good friends will help you to sort out a future filled with opportunities: that does exist, despite all fears. It may not be the one you wish for; but it may also hold unimagined opportunities, including other – and happier – relationships.

H. THERE ARE PLENTY MORE FISH IN THE SEA

And there are, there are – but are you sure you want another fish? Most of us could live happily either as single people, or as one of a pair: in these days of serial monogamy, many of us spend time alternating between these two states. About one-quarter of the households in Britain consist of one person, while in the '80s and '90s there has been a steady increase in the number of never-married single mothers, and of single parents in general.

1. LEARNING FROM THE BAD ONES

Many of the women to whom I talked thought they had only learned about having happy relationships, by having had unhappy ones first – though none of them seemed to have made the classic mistake of bouncing straight from one relationship into another. All of them had been able to find some space for themselves between affairs, and most of them mentioned that space as a healing and positive part of their lives.

2. ALONE AGAIN

"When Luke left, I had time to enjoy myself again, after years of trying to be part of someone else's rhythms," said Kate. *"I had time to see what had gone wrong*

between us – and I decided that I was done with the artists of this world and their self-centredness. I think I worked out how to outgrow my wish to be involved in someone else's creativity, and to see my own world and the people in it as worthwhile."

"Lots of people have a fear of being alone," Sue observed. *"Sometimes, sadly, they find that a sense of grievance makes a good companion – but they may surprise themselves with the discovery of their own companionship, and their own strengths in solitude."* And Claire believes that unrealistic expectations are often caused by a lack of self-confidence, cured by spending time alone.

Being single, after all, isn't some sort of dreadful imprisonment, and most people can find a great pleasure in fending for themselves. But if women frequently report enjoying the time after – or between – relationships, men may have a rather different time of it. A recent study of professional men and women in Britain suggested that women's careers are stimulated into increased success by marriage breakdown, and women generally reported increased levels of motivation. Men, however, often achieve less, feel less motivated and generally are adversely affected by divorce. And another study of divorce in Britain showed that more than half the men interviewed regretted not staying with their ex-wives, while only about a quarter of the women shared that regret.

I. SHAKE HANDS FOREVER?

So, where does that leave you, and the decision that you need to make? Well, Sue firmly believes that you'll know what you should do, if you listen closely enough and carefully enough to your feelings. *"I think people do know in their heart of hearts if they really* want *it to work out,"* she said. *"If you do want it to, then you put up with the knots in the wood; you tolerate what can't be changed. If you* don't *want it to work, then you will fight against everything – your own convenience and peace of mind; your practical best interests; anything, really – to destroy it."*

If one of you wants to maintain the relationship and the other wants it ended, then it will surely end: no-one can sustain a relationship single-handed. If you both try – and if you both want it to continue – then it stands an excellent chance of survival. But the most important question of survival has to – ought to – lie in your own sense of happiness. Life is not a rehearsal – this is *it*, and finding a way to express loving-kindness to ourselves as well as others is an unbeatable priority.

Celebrating Love

In my heart
Within your heart
Is home.
Is peace.
Is quiet.

Eugene O'Neill

Chapter Seven

CELEBRATING LOVE

How good are you at celebrating? How often do you make sure your partner knows about the positive feelings you have for them?

We all know from our own experience just how good it is to be valued – and to be *told* that we are valued. We know that it doesn't take much effort to make a colleague glow with pleasure, or a child feel valued and important; and it's not difficult to thank a friend for support. So why is it hard to remember to praise and celebrate your partner for their good qualities, too?

Maybe we forget that it's needed; perhaps we become too self-absorbed, or just lazy. Maybe we begin to take our partners and their good qualities too much for granted – or we assume that, since they know us so intimately, they must also be able to read our minds, and don't need to be told how much we appreciate and value them. But they do. We often bring an alarmingly accurate precision to the enumerations which begin "the trouble with you is . . ." and a much less confidently practised one to "the wonderful things about you are . . ." or even "I love you because . . ."

A. Taking Time And Care

The need for affirmation (you're doing a wonderful job), for stroking (you're lovable and loved) and for reassurance (I love you and will continue to do so) is a universal one in our culture, and the opportunities to express and exchange these sentiments in positive and life-enhancing ways are present in every intimate partnership. It's a sadly bleak relationship that doesn't include regular opportunities for expressing affection, and yet many people find it very difficult to do just that. If your relationship needs more expressed affection, ask yourself – and ask your partner – how you can best begin to enhance this level of communication, together.

1. EXPRESSING AND RECEIVING AFFECTION

The most important thing to remember is that the way you express and receive affection together can't be determined by someone else; only by you and what feeds your particular personalities and emotional needs. Maybe, for example, you don't feel comfortable about public displays of physical affection. Well, you don't *have* to kiss and cuddle in front of other people if you don't want to: there are lots of other methods of acknowledging the bond between the two of you, and many of them – however subtle – are just as plain a public announcement to your friends.

"If I were going to be envious of another relationship," said Sue, *"it would be of two of my friends who are married but don't live together. And yes, I envy their particular combination of separateness and togetherness, but what I most admire is their endless interest in each other, when they're together or when they're apart. They talk of each other with such admiration and respect."*

2. DEMONSTRATING RESPECT

Respect has been very much the keynote of all the interviews I conducted for this book. Every couple, and most individuals, mentioned it as the most necessary 'given' for continuing happiness, and most returned to it when discussing their observations of other apparently happy, and apparently unhappy relationships.

"Good manners and thoughtfulness keep most things going," Robin observed, *"and I admire those qualities in Brian, together with his loyalty and honesty." "I think I'm a good picker,"* laughed Eileen, *"because as it's turned out, Michael is the anchor of my life, and I have unlimited respect for him." "Chris and I are equal partners and very good friends,"* explained Claire, *"but above all we respect each other."* And that respect – the bedrock of these successful relationships, it seems – is openly acknowledged, and openly expressed.

B. The Signals Of Affection

1. SEXUAL SIGNALS

Sex is often used by couples as a 'signal of affection' – which is fine as far as it goes, but that's seldom far enough for daily life, especially if the particular passion of sexual desire fades, as it usually does over time. So if you always use love-making as the time around when you cuddle and stroke and talk with tenderness, try translating some of that affection to situations which are not sexually specific, as well.

2. AFFECTIONATE GESTURES

Sometimes it's easier for men to compliment women, just because the 'fact' that women like to receive compliments is an accepted truth. And women who expect men to be the strong ones may well not see a need for affirmation in their partners. Sarah, for example, used to expect men to be very strong and so she tended to see them only in that way: *"Now, though, I tend to see their vulnerability more clearly. So I also tend to treat them as people in need of the same things as me."*

Some women believe that their partners don't welcome affectionate gestures. *"He hates what he calls 'lovey-dovey' talk,"* said one woman. Often, it's the in-public/in-private angle that's the real issue, or simply lack of practice. So don't impose your ideas, or swamp your reluctant partner: let them help to determine your guidelines.

3. I LIKE IT WHEN . . .

It is, however, important to know what *you'd* like. Knowing this not only helps you to ask for it when you feel in need of a kiss, a cuddle or a smile, but it also helps you to ask, sense and give your partner what they want, as well. The expressions of affection that you treasure mightn't be the same ones your partner finds nourishing, but it might be a good place to start from, if you live with someone who's unused to demonstrative behaviour. As with any aspect of a relationship, what pleases you may not please your partner – and since you're looking for ways to give another person pleasure by acknowledging their worth to you, you'll need to concentrate on what works for them.

Don't only praise your partner's virtues and strengths; remember to praise them when they get it 'right' for you. *"I like it when you say I look good"*; *"I felt terrific when you telephoned me today – it cheered me up a lot"*; *"I loved finding that note from you – I smiled about it all morning"*; these are all ways to say that you've noticed.

C. Cut Down The Criticisms

As well as seeking positive ways of expressing affection, it's also important to cut down on the negative ones. Lots of people would describe their partner as their best friend: sadly, though, many of us forget to treat our partners as if that were true.

1. PUBLIC EMBARRASSMENT

How many times have you witnessed one partner nagging the other in public – about the way they dress, say, or their weight, or their table manners – which leaves the unpleasant scent of belittlement in the air? If your best friend chewed noisily or wore their shirt hanging out, you'd be much more likely to bite your tongue than to criticise them, especially in front of others – and few of us have the resilience or the patience to respond positively to public nagging.

2. A STRUGGLE FOR POWER

"I often see a highly confrontational style being played out amongst young couples," said Erica. *"It looks like a competition to see whose priorities are the more important; a merciless battle for power, with no thought of negotiation or compromise or even of normal good manners. I don't know how long affection can last in that atmosphere."* If your partner is very critical of you, you'll know how it can wear down positive feelings: if you are the critical one, try deliberately avoiding all criticism for just seven days, and see if there's a different atmosphere for you both.

D. DEALING WITH THE BOREDOM FACTOR

Loving relationships are as subject to the boredom factor as any – especially if they have lasted for long periods of time. If this is the case for you, finding new ways to celebrate and enjoy life with your partner is especially important. Putting back some moments of romance into busy, practical working routines might feel a bit silly initially – but if you can find some strategies with which you're comfortable, the reassurance and excitement which can be generated will go a long way.

1. MAKE THE TIME FOR IT

Despite the pressures and demands of busy lives, we nevertheless tend to make time for the things we truly value. Making time to surprise or please your partner – or simply making time for them at all – is an important first step.

2. CHOOSING YOUR MOMENT

If you can afford to get away alone together for a weekend or a longer break, that's terrific – but don't allow financial or practical difficulties to prevent your finding an alternative. Even just persuading a friend to babysit for you one evening, and spending the time alone together, can be a new beginning.

3. PUT BACK A LITTLE ROMANCE

What used to work best for the two of you, in the early days of your relationship? If your sex life has been sabotaged by babies and familiarity, try finding ways to re-create sexual excitement and passion – there are lots of books and videos from which to glean ideas.

E. Ways Of Loving

There are lots of additional ways to express affection: you might start by looking at the following list. How often do you and your partner use any of them? Which ones do you initiate? Are there any you would like to add? Are there any you'd like your partner to add to their repertoire? Are there any others you use together? Are you receptive to expressions of affection from your partner? Do you respond with warmth and reciprocal affection?

Try one or two new ones every day for a week – and see if it feels good to do that. You have only your inhibitions to lose!

- holding hands
- patting or stroking each other
- putting your arms round each other
- cuddling
- kissing when you meet and part
- kissing first thing in the morning and last thing at night
- calling each other pet names in private
- sharing private games and jokes
- talking to each other without distraction for half an hour
- looking at each other whilst you talk
- talking on the telephone during the day for a brief chat
- writing affectionate or loving notes

- giving each other space and time alone
- sharing an interest or hobby
- giving unexpected presents – it's the thought behind it, not the cost, that's the point

F. THROUGH LOVE'S EYES

Have you ever written a love poem? And if not, why not? Don't dismiss the idea as a piece of adolescent whimsy better suited to the young and foolish – thinking about why you love your partner is a rewarding and revealing exercise, and turning that into a poem can be great fun. One couple who've been married for seventeen years began their love affair with poetry, and continue it each year with a poem from each of them, on the anniversary of the day they met. Sometimes the poems identify a theme for the year that's past, and others are more directly expressive of appreciation and tenderness.

One old one reads in part:

"This year I celebrated
one baby boy
two rooms decorated
three finished tapestries
and beating you at tennis
four weeks running"

Try one your way.

Or write an advertisement for your partner, praising them and recommending their good qualities to the world.

Or make a list of the reasons why you fell in love with your partner in the first place, and the reasons why you love them still.

Or plan to spend an evening alone with your partner, every week for a month. Don't watch television: treat it like a date and be together, be there for each other, and talk. Make it special for each other.

Try it now. This is as good a time as any, isn't it?

Appendices

Appendix One

Helpful Organisations

BRITISH ASSOCIATION FOR COUNSELLING compiles and publishes a directory of counselling organisations and of individual counsellors, and one for your area can be had free (send SAE) from 1 Regent Place, Rugby, CV21 2PJ; telephone (0788) 578328.

NATIONAL ASSOCIATION OF MEDIATION AND CONCILIATION SERVICES offers help to couples going through separation or divorce, usually through three counselling sessions; contact them at The Shaftesbury Centre, Percy Street, Swindon SN2 2AZ; telephone (0793) 514055.

RELATE (the renamed Marriage Guidance Council) offers professional counselling to those in relationships. Your telephone book will list your nearest office, or you could contact the national headquarters at Herbert Gray College, Little Church Street, Rugby, CV21 3AP; telephone (0788) 573241.

Appendix Two

INTERESTING FURTHER READING

Anatomy of Love:
a natural history of adultery, monogamy and divorce
Helen Fisher (Simon & Schuster 1992)

Brainsex
Anne Moir and David Jessel (Mandarin 1989)

From This Day Forward:
an anthology of marriage
Bel Mooney (John Murray 1989)

The Relate Guide To Better Relationships
Sarah Litvinoff (Vermilion 1992)

Wanting Everything
Dorothy Rowe (Fontana 1992)

Staying Together

We Two
Roger Housden and Chloe Goodchild (Aquarian 1992)

A Woman in Your Own Right: assertiveness and you
Anne Dickson (Quartet 1982)

You Just Don't Understand: women and men in conversation
Deborah Tannen (Virago 1992)

The End

There is nothing lovelier than when man and wife keep house together with like heart and will. Their foes resent it and their friends rejoice, but the truth of it all is known only to them.

Odysseus talking to Nausicaa,
in Homer's *Odyssey*

Sometimes our best efforts do not go amiss; sometimes we do as we meant to. The sun will sometimes melt a field of sorrow that seemed hard frozen: may it happen for you.

Sheenagh Pugh

Other Books In The Piccadilly Pointers Series

ADVENTURE UNLIMITED
Living and Working Abroad
by Suzanne Askham

ARE YOU READY YET?
Preparing for a New Relationship
by John Gordon

FINDING THE LOVE OF YOUR LIFE
Using Dating Agencies and Ads
by Linda Sonntag

INSIDE MEN'S MINDS
Young Men Talk
by Nick Fisher

STAYING TOGETHER

PROBLEM PERIODS
Causes, Symptoms, and Relief
by Dr Caroline Shreeve

SINGLE AGAIN
Living Alone and Liking It
by Anita Naik

STRONG ENOUGH FOR TWO
Women Taking the Strain in a Relationship
by Liz Roberts

WHAT WORRIES WOMEN MOST
Your Medical Questions Answered
by Dr Sarah Brewer